unbreakable

The Autobiography of the
Life of Susan Stewart

CONCLUSIO
HOUSE PUBLISHING

Printed in Canada

First Printing, 2015

ISBN 978-0-9938420-3-0

Conclusio House Publishing
Brampton, Ontario

www.conclusiohouse.com

http://suestewart.ca

Disclaimer: Except for those who have given their expressed permission, all names and identifiable characteristics have been changed to protect the true identities of individuals mentioned in this book.

*To the One who continually comforts
my soul throughout this journey.*

For His glory...

Acknowledgements

To my father, mother, sister, nephew, and niece, thank you for never leaving my side and being a constant support to me. You have helped me get to where I am today.

Special thanks to Kerri-Ann Haye-Donawa, my writer and editor, for helping me to capture my story, and for chronicling my memories in this book to share with the world.

My deepest gratitude to those who donated financially to the completion of this project, namely Mr. James P. Holmes and Mrs. Patricia A. Holmes, Derrydale Golf Course, Jeanie's Market, Original Jerk, Joy McNichol, Tonya Tatti, Chantal St. Martin, Dr. M. Goldstein Dentistry Professional Corporation, Alisha Tatham and Kalisha Keane of Love Live and Hoop.

A warm thank you to Herbie and Stephanie Kuhn, Tammy Sutton-Brown, Hans Rothenbuhler, Pat and Kristin Presley, David and Alysaa Presley, the Ortlip family, Tanya Hockman, George MaWherter, Kelsey MacWherter, Stephanie McPherson, Jordan Fairback, Dr. Greg Linville, Brenda Stevens, Howard Taylor, Suzie Ward Thomas, Stephen and Susan Moroney, Dennis and Elsa Stern and family, Andre Thornton, John and Cindy Rothenbuler, Ann Rothenbuhler, Susie and Bill Traux, Oleta Payne, David and Ruth Hudson, Nora Hancock, Lori Wynn, Dr. Jason Carthen, Ann Marie Thuss, Gloria Hanam, Jackie Nugent, Andrea Levy-Hudson, Hopelyn West-Smith, Fergy Neves, the Binger Family, Barry and Beverly Graham, Catherine Holland, Charmaine Crooks, Hayley Wickenheiser, Christine Stapleton, Dianne Norman, Opal McKenzie, Pastor Gary and Debra Martin, Lamar and Helen Stewart, Velma Moore-Pruitt, Pastor Lennox and Dorett Walker, Cary and Amelia Kaplan, Dr. Ivan Joseph, Michele Belanger, Shirlene Mclean, Angie MacDonald, Betty Baculo, Andre Hyman, Orlando Bowen, Chuck Ealey, Chris Critelli, Kathy Shields,

Michelle O'Keefe, Dana McKiel, Denise Perrier, Catherine Amara, Jacqueline Green, Hyacinth King, Emily and Joel Flett, Cathy Morenzie, Lorna Lewis, Semone Johnson, Del Marie Brandt, Jerome Innis, Alyona Lewis, Petula Wilmot Chambers, Charmaine Smith, Kelly Boucher, Chris Bosh, Donavon Bailey, Natalie Brown, Michael (Pinball) Clemons, Judith Gayle, Alice Simpson (WNBA Chaplain), Stephanie Zonars, Shauna Stone, Everton Webb, Jestina Mitchell, Malcolm Lewis, Carmen Shann, and Stafford Shann.

To the many aunts, uncles, cousins, my godson, longtime family friends, and family members, there are too many to mention, thank you!

Thank you to the following institutions, businesses, teams, and organizations: The Fellowship of Christian Athletes; Athletes in Action; First Friend Church; Praise Cathedral Worship Centre, Peel-Halton Acquired Brain Injury Services; Recovery to Discovery Brain Injury Association of Peel-Halton; Coalition for Persons with Disabilities; True Light Christian Church; Parkside Church; 100 Huntley Street; Laurentian Lady Vees Alumni Basketball; Cosmo Sports; Sports Marketing; JUEL of Ontario; Mississauga Sports Council; One Voice, One Team (Get S.W.O.L.E); Mississauga Mayor Taskforce on Sport (2010); Canadian Interuniversity Sport; Vere Technical Alumni (Jamaican); Mississauga News; Rogers TV Mississauga; National Post (Newspaper); CBC Radio (Toronto); The Share (Newspaper); Canton Repository (Newspaper); Total U Hair Care; Edwin Shaw Rehabilitation Institute (Akron, OH); Community Clubhouse for Brain Injury; Middlefield Swiss Cheese (Middlefield, OH); Salon Paradise; JABEZ Gospel Music; Truth for Life; The Chapel (Green Campus, Akron, OH); Mercy Medical Hospital; Malone College; Trillium Health Centre; Toronto Rehabilitation Institute; Credit Valley Hospital; Next Step to Active Living; Streetsville Secondary School; Malone College Women's Basketball Team (2004-05); St. Aloysius Gonzaga Senior Boys' Basketball Team; Mississauga Wolverines Basketball Association; Varsity Blues Women's Basketball Team (2012-13); Toronto Academy Junior Girls' Basketball Team (2013); Ryerson Rams Women's Basketball Team (2011-12); Sheridan Bruins (Trafalgar Campus, Bruin Fitness); York Lions Athletics (Tait Mackenzie Centre); Swiss Selects Girls' Basketball Team (2004-05); Streetsville Secondary Junior Girls' Basketball Team (2007); Windsor Lancer Women's Basketball Program; Ontario University Athletics (OUA); Canadian Interuniversity

Sport (CIS); TransHelp; and Blue and White Taxi.

Thank you, all of you, for your help and support over the years!

Together Everyone Achieves More (T.E.A.M.)

The following people have meant a lot to me during my growth and development as a person. Though they are gone, they are not forgotten.

- Great-Grandmother Hannah Ann Fielding (1981)

- Washington Douglas Green (1993)

- Diana Wilmot Scott (1994)

- Lady Vees Head Coach Peter Ennis (1997)

- Craig Garth Anthony Redwood (1998)

- Dr. James G. King III (2002)

- Lady Vees Teammate Dr. Susan Foy (2003)

- Dalton Miller (2004)

- Lady Vees Teammate Carolyn Swords (2009)

- Lena May Ricketts (2013)

- Aunt Patricia Elaine Redwood (2014)

- Hugh Lindo Harvey (2014)

- Grandmother Ivy Icelyn Harrison (2014)

Table of Contents

Foreword

◇◇

There is something unbreakable about writing the foreword for *Unbreakable*. It will make you miss your appointments. The testimony shared by Susan L. Stewart, a remarkable woman of God, ranks very high amongst the compelling testimonies I have read and witnessed in my forty years of ministry. And trust me, I have encountered many.

This is a book that you will be grateful to read. It will help to develop your faith in God. It will bring you into a closer relationship with God, knowing that He is still in the healing business and that He is the Rock of our Gibraltar. This book will help you to grow in strength, knowing fully well that God, who is with you, will save and protect you because you love and acknowledge Him as Lord (Psalm 91:14). *Unbreakable* will stay with you when you are in the valley and rise with you onto the mountain top. If this were a novel, you would perhaps think the testimonies were unbelievable. But they are real.

We know that even the most gifted athlete must push herself in order to make it onto the high school team, much less onto the professional stage. Susan was named Canada's best female university basketball player in 1992, the year after Laurentian University defended its national title, and it was four years later that she was drafted to the Canadian Summer Olympics team. It was during this time that I personally met

Susan. She was attending Praise Cathedral Worship Centre (*formerly,* Erin Mills Church of God). I had the awesome privilege of baptizing her and becoming her pastor. What an honour it has been! Susan is one of the most faithful and authentic Christians I have met.

Imagine being at the pinnacle of your career, doing what you do best and doing it at the highest level, ignoring God's call on your life. Then when it becomes difficult, and you start to worry about what to do next, God begins to open doors for you. Then, once you have achieved what you have been working towards all your life, suddenly you experience a bad accident that quickly spirals into slurred speech, a coma, and last rites being delivered at your bedside.

This, in essence, is just a short episode of Sue's testimony. When everyone else may have lost hope, Sue did not give up on God. Sue had to figure out how to walk and talk again. Her faith was tested. And she proved God, who in His mercies spared her. Today, her life is a living testimony of what God has done for her and will do for us if we only believe.

Sue shares her testimonies to remind us that God is still God. *Unbreakable* is filled with Sue's real life experiences. After reading *Unbreakable,* you will understand that relying totally on God, instead of focusing on self, is the ultimate way to one's healing. In God you are Unbreakable. Enjoy!

Bishop Lennox Walker
Administrative Bishop, Church of God in Ontario
Senior Pastor, Praise Cathedral Worship Centre

Preface

◇◇

This book was simply an idea for many years. The idea was first implanted during a conversation with the nurses at Toronto Rehab, who mentioned that my story was worth telling. After years of prompting by friends and relatives, I believe the time has finally come to share my journey with you.

This book is about the faithfulness of God. It's about His mercy extended to a life that has been riddled with trials and pain, and that has experienced much victory in spite of. Philippians 1:29 says, *"For it has been granted to you on behalf of Christ, not only to believe in Him, but also to suffer with Him."* Suffering is a necessary part of our journey. We will all suffer, in one way or another. For me it was a life-changing injury, for you it may be a broken marriage, a failed career, various forms of abuse, relational dysfunction, etcetera. But through it all, God has promised to be with us and to never forsake us. Remember that.

As you read my story, may you grasp the reality that you too can overcome every obstacle that comes across your path. Life may not always be a smooth course, it may not always feel good, but you have within you the power to navigate the rough places and come out a champion. Despite the challenges you are facing, decide to press through your difficulties and reach your very highest potential. May your faith be strengthened and your heart encouraged by this my autobiography.

With love,

Susan Stewart

PART ONE
The Journey

CHAPTER ONE
Growing Up Suburban

November 14, 1969 was a cool, sunny day in Toronto, Ontario. There was no autumn rain. No early snow. All that filled the air were gentle rays of sunshine and the chill that marked winter's approach. It was a perfect day for a champion to be born. They named me Susan Laurrine Stewart.

I was the firstborn for my parents, Winston and Nona Stewart, both immigrants to Canada from Clarendon, Jamaica where they met in their youth and fell in love. Eighteen months after my happy arrival, as though my birth had stirred some uncontainable excitement, my sister, Dian, was born. It was then, in 1971, that I met my lifelong best-friend. I liked my sister instantly. The mere months that separated our births only worked to my mother's advantage since she valued familial bonds above everything else and saw to it, as much as she was able, that Dian and I became best friends long before we were old enough to choose differently. Mom was the relational glue in our home and she never grew weary of her role.

My parents raised us in Mississauga, Ontario in a charming, suburban neighbourhood decked with manicured lawns and colourful playgrounds. It was structurally designed for the middle-class family. And Dian and I revelled in happy and normal childhood experiences, as far as the words *happy* and *normal* extend. We lived in a comfortable home with parents who worked hard to ensure that we had whatever we needed. My mother worked full-time in banking, but she also sold Fuller Brush and Tupperware products on the side to make extra money. My father, on the other hand, worked on the assembly line at Ford Motors on a shift rotation cycle. To me, he was always at work, leaving my mother and great-grandmother to take care of the home. But he was an excellent provider. His personal glory was unveiled in him working arduously to make sure his family had a good life. And we enjoyed that life, all of us together—Mom working two jobs and Dad working as many hours as he could acquire.

My maternal great-grandmother, Hannah Fielding, shared our home and helped to raise Dian and me. She was like our live-in caregiver who took great pride in training us according to the principles of her generation and her faith. She was a staunch Seventh Day Adventist who taught us about the importance of church and going to Sunday school. She considered it her personal responsibility to ensure that we had God in us from a very young age. "I want to make sure you girls never stray," she would say. She was never nonchalant about her role in our lives. She knew we were an extension of her bloodline, so she made sure she instilled cultural awareness, generational customs, and religion in us at every turn. And though strict, my West Indian upbringing brought with it laughter and tough lessons that only seasoned my sense of identity the more.

I was a tomboy, and that natural bent in my personality

further distinguished me in my young years. I loved the outdoors so much that I spent as much time outside as I did inside, playing game after game. I think the outdoors helped to carve out the athlete in me because it wasn't too long into my childhood before I realized that playing, for me, wasn't just about having fun, but also about the joy of winning.

I was both fun-loving and athletic. And the older I became, the more those qualities grew within me. Somehow I knew I was a winner, even way back then. I also knew that positivity was something I needed to guard with all my strength, and so from my innocent hide-and-seek days, I made it a point of my duty to stay on top of my happiness at all times.

———— ◇◇ ————

When the time finally came for me to venture outside of the home for school, I was sent to Thorn Lodge Public School, a petite, inviting structure, neatly positioned as a statement piece within the confines of our neighbourhood. I revelled in the social outlet that going to school provided, but academically, I was only an average student. That's because my passion wasn't for books or achieving high grades; it was for having fun. Fun was the absolute meaning of life in my youthful years, and I lived by that code to the fullest extent—fun with the kids at school, fun with the kids on my street, and fun everywhere else in between. And on top of that, I played every sport imaginable.

It's no wonder then that I had a lot of friends growing up, some may say too many. But I wouldn't have had it any other way. I was a people-person, an extrovert by nature; it flowed in my blood and mingled with everything I did. If someone wasn't smiling when they were in my presence, I felt it was my responsibility to lighten the mood in order to create a smile and, more often, a laugh.

My parents were never surprised by my antics. They knew the person I was and what I was capable of. They even knew, long before I confessed to it, that I was responsible for the blitz of doorbell-ringing pranks that my friends and I started in our neighbourhood. We found it most entertaining to run up to random houses on our streets, ring the doorbell, and then run away as fast as we could. Needless to say that no one else was quite as amused as we were, our parents least of all. But making mischief wasn't all we did. We would also routinely gather in each other's basements and watch movies. These were the moments of bonding that shaped us for years to come.

The summer months were populated by trips to the beach, Niagara Falls, and visits from out-of-town family members. My mother made sure that we had a close relationship with our extended family at all times. As such, it was the norm to have our cousins, and aunts come to visit with us. It was *family* that was our first family value, not riches, not fame, but family and love.

One particularly warm summer day, as I strolled briskly along the sidewalks of Homelands Drive, I met a spunky girl who was also out for a walk. We were both around eight years old.

"I'm Michelle," she introduced herself.

"I'm Sue," I said with a smile.

As we got acquainted that day, we realized that we had lived in the same neighbourhood for all our lives to that point, but had never met. I couldn't help but feel like there was something electric about our paths crossing that day. Our friendship was born instantly, as though we had always known each other and had always been friends. We were alike in many ways, but yet different enough to blend beautifully like the colours in a rainbow. That summer, Michelle, Dian, and I became inseparable. We each knew what the other was thinking, and appreciated the different flavours we each brought to our little circle.

Summer was a time of mischief for me. Somehow the warm sunshine invited me to do things that other little girls didn't find appealing. Like the day I decided to hold on to the seat of Michelle's bicycle as she rode down the street, while following on my skateboard. The feeling was exhilarating as the wind whipped faster and faster around my face.

"Go faster!" I called out to her, laughing. "Faster! Faster!" I threw my head back in sheer enjoyment as Michelle pedalled as fast as she could.

It was the perfect thrill, until suddenly, the front wheel of her bike hit a rock, jamming the progress, and sending me flying into the air. I flew over the bicycle and landed face-first onto the sidewalk. The taste of blood filled my mouth as my lip split open and painted my teeth red. You'd think the pain would've changed the course of my actions, or at least curbed my addiction to antics, but it didn't, not even a little. I was back out within a day, riding my bike at full speed down the sidewalk. My burning lip was merely an afterthought as I demonstrated another stunt for my friends and onlookers.

I can still remember the day when Robert—a boy from my neighbourhood—and I got into a disagreement. As we argued, he got so angry that he threw a rock at me and it split my lip, again, leaving a scar that is still present to this day. My ability to get into trouble made life interesting, and my accident-prone tendency caused my parents to have to rush me to the hospital to get treated on multiple occasions.

◇◇

Our parents allowed us to play within the boundaries of our immediate neighbourhood, but we were strictly forbidden to venture onto the main streets. Somehow for Michelle and me, the Woodchester Mall, which sat just beyond the confines of our neighbourhood, represented the greatest adventure two eight-year-olds could ever have. It was a ten- to fifteen-minute bike ride to the mall, much further than either of us had ever travelled on our own.

"Michelle, let's ride over to the mall and check it out." I was eager to go without our parents.

"Are you crazy? What if we get caught, huh?" Michelle knew the rules as well as I did.

"We won't." I assured her. "Let's just wait until our parents go to work tomorrow. They'll never know we went."

It sounded like an easy enough plan, so the next day while our parents were at work we rode over to the mall for a day of exploration. Whether it was by fate or by chance, my father just happened to drive by the mall soon after we had arrived.

"What are you girls doing so far out of the neighbourhood?" he asked, half rhetorically and half demanding an explanation. He was angry.

We stood there for a few moments like deer in headlights; neither of us could respond. My father, not getting an answer to his question, demanded that we return home right away.

Michelle and I cried all the way home because we were both terrified by the fact that we had been caught, and also seriously afraid of the consequences that were awaiting us. That night, we were both scolded and grounded for our decision to go to the mall without a chaperone. And though I never made that mistake again, I made many others.

It wasn't long before my tomboy bent became more real. I soon began to feel like a boy living in a girl's body. I couldn't understand why it wasn't okay for me to do the things that the boys did. Like one day when I was invited to go swimming in the neighbour's backyard. My swimwear of choice was a pair of shorts and no top. After all, why couldn't I go swimming topless? As I ran to the door with my towel in hand, my parents stopped me.

"Where do you think you're going dressed like that?"

"Swimming!" I replied with excitement.

"Not like that, you aren't!" Then came the first lecture on sexuality that I would receive from my parents. "You're a girl, Sue, and girls are different from boys."

"But why can't I go swimming in just my shorts?" I was confused.

They were determined to teach me what it meant to be a girl and how to behave like a girl was supposed to behave. Those years of moulding my sense of self were difficult for me because I had always hated the feeling of restraint. I didn't see my gender as a limitation. I saw being a girl as powerful. So, though I eventually conformed my clothing style to meet my parents' desire, on the inside my free spirit remained unleashed.

CHAPTER TWO
Hello, Basketball

I started high school in 1984. The school I attended — Streetsville Secondary—was small, and only had about five hundred students at the time. I was a tall, skinny black girl in a school that only had a handful of black students, so I stood out quite easily in a crowd. But I didn't mind because standing out has never bothered me.

I was an independent child, and even had my own paper route delivering the *Mississauga News* and flyers in my neighborhood. My personality helped me manage change well, so I soon acclimated to my new environment. In fact, I relished everything high school had to offer. There was one thing in particular that lured me to school every day, and that was the competition that high school sports offered. The sheer excitement of trying out for a team and then being selected was deeply rewarding. I saw the opportunity to try out as a privilege, so I tried out for the basketball team as soon as I started grade nine. It was then that my love for the game was born and there where it developed into a full-blown passion.

After trying out, I was amongst the elite group of girls who were selected to be a part of the girls' team. My basketball career begun that day. It didn't take long before I realized that I was good at it. I had excitement for the game, and it drove me.

I loved watching my idol, Magic Johnson, succeed, and I often imagined myself succeeding in basketball the way he did. The power of my imagination lured me to become better, to show up early, and to leave late. It was evident that I had what it took to be a real champion.

Throughout my high school years, my popularity bloomed as a consequence of me being on the basketball team. There was one particular game in which I scored forty points in a home game. I was the talk of the school for days following that game. Everyone knew my name, and I was well-liked. That social element of high school mixed with the maturity that came from being with the older kids made high school altogether fun.

My popularity was particularly attractive to the boys. However, though the boys were indeed good looking, and some quite interesting, no one guy was ever interesting enough to pull me away from the game. Although I spent time with boys, here and there, no serious boyfriend ever emerged, except for a close friendship that eventually developed between me and one particular boy.

———————— ◇◇ ————————

High school came with its many challenges, but I didn't let it deter me from working towards my goals. I competed in every sporting event I could. My drive was fuelled by the opportunity to be on multiple teams and interact with many different people—not just the athletes. It was my basketball career that kept me out of trouble; it prevented me from skipping school and chasing boys. It kept me focused on wanting to be among the elite athletes. I wanted to be the best and to play with the best.

During a game at Cawthra Park Secondary School, I was approached by one of the referees who encouraged me to try out for the Toronto club team, Metro Junior Radars. And so I did.

The one thing I wasn't proud of in terms of ideal high school accomplishments was my academic standing. I was merely an average student. Unfortunately, basketball always took precedence over my academics. In fact, I only did what I had to in order to receive the grades necessary to play. It wasn't until the final year of high school that I became serious about my studies. I had scholarship offers from schools in Canada as well as the United States. Of course, I had my eye on the university that I wanted to play for, and that drove me to do better both on the court and in the classroom. That year, I got serious and started to put in the work to improve my grades.

My high school career as an athlete was remarkably successful. During my years at Streetsville Secondary, I was invited to the Top Forty Camp, which was held at Queen's University to showcase the top female basketball players in Ontario. A year later, I played on the Ontario Provincial team in Lethbridge, Alberta. That same year, I was also invited to play for Canada's Senior Women's National Basketball Team's Fall NCAA tour. I also played for the Metro Junior Raiders, a club basketball team in Toronto. And then I played on Canada's Junior National Basketball Team for the FIBA Americas World Championship tournament.

My athletic journey filled me with hope and excitement. It was exhilarating. Being able to travel to the United States for the American tour opened my eyes to the world of opportunities that this game had to offer me. I decided then, while I was still in high school, to pursue the sport with all I had.

As I played the various tournaments, I began to receive recognition for my skills. In fact, it was during a game in Alberta that Peter Ennis of Laurentian University first noticed me. Upon my return home to Ontario, I started to receive letters from Peter Ennis. His compassion for his players and his exceptional people skills stood out to me. But what really made a difference was the time and care he took to visit with my family and connect with my parents in order to recruit me. I felt privileged to be handed the opportunity to play for a coach like Peter Ennis, and so I accepted the offer to attend Laurentian University after high school.

Junior Women's National Basketball Team

CHAPTER THREE
The Lady Vees

Throughout my university career, my friendship groups remained separate and distinct as they had always been. I had my athletic friends from the sports teams around the school, I had my friends from the Caribbean Association on campus—Maria and Marcia, and then there were my outside-of-school friends. At this point, I felt a sense of freedom in the ability to grow and learn outside of family life.

I lived in a single-student residence during my first two years at Laurentian University. Once again, the newness of my environment was both refreshing and inviting to me. I was an extrovert at heart. I frequented the pub on campus and most of the other social activities that the school hosted because music was one of my great loves and so was dancing.

"Work hard, play hard," that was the motto I lived by. As an athlete, I had basketball games in many different cities and rubbed shoulders with various sports teams. Hence, it was inevitable that I'd meet a variety of male players. My interest in boys began to grow as I had the opportunity to spend more time with them off the court. Though I never went home with any of the guys I met, I had fun befriending them and partying with them. Needless to say, since I was deeply involved in the athletic culture, I was exposed to guys with muscular bodies and charming personalities. And they were used to getting attention as much as I was.

My first serious relationship in university was with a basketball player on the men's team. My only relationship prior to that was in high school with a premier basketball player in my city. We had gone out a few times back then, but our relationship didn't last beyond high school. So I welcomed the thought of this new relationship.

I really liked having a 'real' boyfriend because it was my official welcome to womanhood. I was no longer the tomboy I was in high school. I had developed into a woman who enjoyed the male attention I was receiving. Our relationship lasted for about a year until we decided to go our separate ways. He was my introduction to the flutters that romantic relationships give.

It was during this time that I was fortunate enough to meet Shirlene, who is still one of my best friends. She was a sister to me on campus, and would look out for me to ensure that I didn't do anything stupid enough to seriously jeopardize my basketball career.

———— ◇◇◇ ————

Laurentian University was instrumental in grooming the champion in me. I played five years of basketball there, and was a five-time Ontario University Athletics (OUA) provincial champion, two-time Canadian Interuniversity Sport (CIS) national champion, and three-time CIS bronze medalist during my tenure. I was even named CIS best female university player in 1992 after helping Laurentian University defend its national title. Somehow, our coach, Peter, was able to deal with the many different personalities on our team with great mastery. He attracted champions and he made them better.

Peter was intense but fun. He'd bring in blocking dummies and put U of T shirts on them, and hammer us under the basket. We had intense two-minute drills. His belief was that our games would never be as hard as our practices because no one would ever push us harder than our teammates would. According to our team therapist, Nicole, he was pumped when the rookies showed up. He would train us in a way that he believed would prevent our opponents from ever getting relief, because if five of us subbed off, the five who subbed on would be just as punishing. Then there were those sessions in the pool whenever we got a little tired of the gym. He trained us hard, and it was all a part of his desire to build mental toughness in his girls. His number one priority was to foster a playing style that was big, strong, and fast, and to develop girls who could move the ball well up the court, around the perimeter, and inside the key. We quickly got used to physical contact, running the floor, barking orders, and going after rebounds. Peter would chastise us if we were being "friction phantoms," a term that described anyone who he felt was not satisfactorily keeping in touch with him. He wanted to know what was going on with his players—who they were, what they were up to, who they were hanging with, how school was going, how their families were doing. He took care of the whole person. He and Angie, the assistant coach, were like parents to us girls, and often he would have Angie ask us the tough questions and then relay the information back to him.

I was always proud of being one of Peter's players. I completely immersed myself in the culture of Laurentian athletics and the university on a whole. I rarely complained about anything; I was too busy being happy. Some say that I was a true ambassador for the team, always respectful and friendly. According to Nicole, I was one of Peter's biggest ever recruiting achievements. She said she was working in the Athletic Office during my final year of high school while he was corresponding with me, and a few other prospects—Di, Nana, Gully, Martha, and Trish. She told me that he was excited at the thought of having any of us, never mind all of us, join the team.

"You especially were a pretty big draw," she said. "You and Gully were the rocks of the team, along with Shirl."

I never wavered in my loyalty to Peter, Angie, and the team. But I also always had fun. There was one time when I went to the local pub with my friends. I somehow became the centre of attention as I took over the floor dancing in my overalls, which I then undid while still on the dance floor. Of course they ended up revealing my underclothes, which at the time were a pair of shorts. It was the highlight of the night.

———— ◇◇ ————

When I entered my final year at Laurentian, we lost some great veteran players, but this brought in some new and exciting rookies to the Lady Vees Basketball program. There was a new flurry of activity on the court. We trained harder than ever before. We trained for two hours at a time, and each practice was designed to grill us into the most physically fit shape of our lives. We did a lot of dry-land training and on-court training. All the pain I endured in training, however, was rewarded when I was given the opportunity to play oversees and represent Canada. My first international trip was to Brazil. It was a world qualifications tournament.

In the space of a few short years, I had gone from the Junior Women's National Team to the World Student Games to the Pan American Games to the Senior Women's National Team. I played for three different coaches on the various national teams, and was the only black female on each team.

In July 1995, at McMaster University, I played the best game of my career against Cuba. Playing at home, surrounded by my friends and family, was exhilarating. My parents watched from the stands, and their excitement oozed through their eyes till it met me on the court. The renowned Herbie Kuhn was the announcer for that game, which made the experience even more amazing. As I won the gold medal that day, I knew I had qualified for the 1996 Atlanta Olympics. I had unfortunately missed the qualifications for the Barcelona Olympics in 1992 and had to start the qualifying process all over again for another four years. So it took me a total of eight years to qualify for the 1996 Atlanta Olympics. That day when I won the gold medal I knew that I had reached the pinnacle of my career to date.

The feeling was unlike anything I had ever felt before. I was fulfilled, excited, grateful, and above all, I was a champion. I couldn't sleep that night. Not even a wink. The exhilaration bounced around in my body, keeping me awake. I had met my goal. I had won all the games that counted, and had made it to the top rung of the ladder of my basketball career—the Olympics.

To commemorate our victory and forever memorialize the event, a group of us on the qualifying team decided to get a tattoo. I chose the Olympic logo with the Canadian maple leaf and torch on top. It was done in full colour on the left side of my chest, above my heart. I loved it. Even now, it reminds me every day of that moment when I reached a milestone in my career. I was now an Olympian.

Chapter Four

The Olympics

———————— ⁖ ————————

The spring of 1996, I returned from Regensdorf, Switzerland, where I was playing with a professional team, to meet the rest of the Canadian team to train for the upcoming summer Olympics. As we prepared for the game, we played matches in Europe and throughout Canada. We trained twice a day for three hours each session. The first thing we did was the beep test to assess our fitness level; it was a rigorous beginning to my Olympic experience. We were matched according to our positions and evaluated based on our performance.

As we prepared for the world stage, we played against many different teams so that we could experience the different playing styles we would encounter. I remember playing against Russia and feeling the sting of the pre-season competition. We won some of our matches easily, but lost miserably in others. By the time the Olympics rolled around, our team entered as seventh in the world. There were twelve countries competing in our sport. Unfortunately, just two weeks before the Olympic games, I was sidelined by a knee injury. I was frustrated, to say the least, as this was the most important moment in my entire career. Nevertheless, I looked forward the games with no less excitement.

I felt like a kid in a candy store throughout the entire flight to Atlanta. I was abuzz, practically bouncing off of everything.

I wonder what it will be like, I thought. *We're good enough to win a medal, but can we take home the gold for Canada?*

When we finally arrived, I was in awe. It was more than I could've imagined. It was like we were in a different world altogether. The preparations they had made for us were elaborate. Everything was free—the food, the salon, the activities, you name it. I took advantage of the opportunity to get my hair done and re-coloured every two days while I was there. We weren't allowed to wear too much of one sponsor's sportswear, so we rotated our sponsor-gifted clothing daily.

The opening ceremony was like walking on *The Wizard of Oz*'s yellow brick road; it was magical. Muhammed Ali lit the torch and received a replacement gold medal for his boxing victory in the 1960 Summer Olympics. Celine Dion sung "The Power of the Dream," accompanied by David Foster on the piano. Gladys Knight sang, "Georgia on My Mind," and the ceremony was officially opened by President Bill Clinton. It was surreal. Every athlete was in tip-top shape, donning perfect bodies and the belief that they would win. I was mesmerized as I watched the screen from where we were waiting. When they called for Canada we were still in the other stadium (there were two stadiums side by side), so we had to run from where we were to get to the main stadium. I laughed with sheer glee as we ran. "Come on, ladies. Faster!" I giggled as I cheered our group forward. *We'd better make it in time.* We did.

Walking across that stadium in Atlanta was one of the proudest moments of my life. Our countrymen in the stands, which included my family and boyfriend of two years at the time, cheered as we walked by, and we waved with patriotic pride. Our eyes glistened with tears.

Yes, I am an Olympic athlete. Me, Sue.

We were a better team than we showed our opponents and the world. For some reason, our team became disjointed by the time we played our first game. We tanked. We just couldn't score. We didn't play the way we were used to playing, which was frustrating. Because of my injury, I had to sit and watch my team struggle throughout each game. I felt helpless, and did the best I could with the time I had on the court.

It all came apart after our loss to Italy. One loss after the next, our Olympic dreams came to a close. We played seven games in Atlanta—against Japan, Russia, China, Italy, Brazil, South Korea, and Congo—and lost most of them. Our last game was against Congo, which we won to place eleventh of twelve in rank.

The results were disappointing. In fact, the entire experience had gone from euphoric to bittersweet. On the one hand, it was thrilling to be a part of such an amazing time in history. But on the other hand, it was devastating because we were unable to capitalize on the experience as a team. We couldn't pull it together enough to score the points and win the games we needed to win to be the champions. By the end of our segment, I was so tired and crushed by the results that I decided not to stay for the closing ceremonies. After our last game, I caught a flight and went straight home to Canada. I was fatigued and had an injured left knee.

After returning home, I went to see my family doctor for

my regular physical examination. He asked me the routine questions.

"Are you sexually active?"

"Yes."

"Do you think you could be pregnant right now?"

"No, I don't think I am," I answered.

It wasn't that we were taking the precautionary measures to ensure that I wouldn't conceive, but more so that I didn't believe that I had. As was routine, my doctor then asked me to take a pregnancy test, just to be sure.

To my surprise, it came back positive.

I was so naïve at that point in my life that I didn't even consider the possibility of this happening. I was so busy controlling my basketball career that I had not paid attention to the possible repercussions of being in a long-term sexual relationship. Unfortunately, I wasn't very open about my relationships either, so I didn't receive the valuable advice I needed.

"Sue, you're pregnant."

"But..." His words sent shockwaves through my body.

What am I going to do?

I was disappointed in myself for not being more careful. After living a relatively trouble-free life, I had let myself down. The critic in my head yelled at me. I let myself 'have it,' mentally. Everyone could tell something was wrong with me, but I didn't tell anyone except my parents what I had discovered. I was a twenty-six-year-old unemployed, unmarried woman who was pregnant with her first child. It didn't help that the Jamaican culture that I was from housed an inherent judgmental perspective towards matters like these. I didn't want to deal with their questions. Not to mention my own confusion about how I would support my child since I didn't have a job.

My boyfriend at the time was surprisingly supportive when I shared the news with him. We both knew that our relationship was not headed towards marriage. We were not in love, per se, but we were fond of each other, enough to have committed to each other for the past two years. Yes, he had a job and he was good guy, but we weren't quite ready to share a child. I was forced to weigh my options and consider the consequences.

Should I carry the baby to term? How will I raise him or her? What about basketball?

I could hear my heart aching with the possibility of making the wrong decision. I pondered and worried and cried, then I made my decision. I decided to terminate the pregnancy. I wasn't ready to be a mother. My partner came with me to the hospital that day and waited for me to complete the procedure.

A few months later, our relationship ended.

The months following my abortion marked the first time I had felt shame so strongly. I couldn't escape it. I was at the edge of a nervous breakdown as the weight of my guilt consumed me. I didn't realize the effect the procedure would have on my mind and my emotions. I became bound by the emotional pain that resulted.

I still live with the memory of that decision today, though not with the shame. And as I look back, I realize that the pregnancy might have accounted for why I wasn't up to par physically, and may have contributed to me not being able to play my best at the Olympics that year.

SUE STEWART # 7

Canadian
Olympic
Committee

Comité
olympique
canadien

English   Français

CHAPTER FIVE
Life After Atlanta

By 1997, the Olympics had become a fond memory that represented everything I had wanted to accomplish athletically up to that point. I finished playing oversees and returned home. I was exhausted with playing in Europe and was ready to explore what the United States had to offer. They had just introduced the American Basketball League, and I desperately wanted to play for them. I naturally felt drawn to the ABL because it was birthed out of the 1996 Olympics. In fact, they started by signing a majority of the players from team USA's women's basketball team that had competed in Atlanta. My hopes to play for the ABL quickly abated when the league disintegrated in 1998. They only lasted for about two seasons before suddenly declaring bankruptcy. Thankfully, the Women's National Basketball Association (WNBA) had also been introduced the year prior.

I hadn't prepared for life after basketball. Basketball had been my entire life for so many years that I didn't really think that life existed outside of it. In the United States, they encourage players to go into coaching because there are many opportunities, but those same opportunities are not as plentiful in Canada. Hence, there were no jobs available in coaching for young athletes like myself. My world was jittery. I needed to play for a league, and quickly.

I returned to the national team to try to take my mind off the Olympics. And one particular day after a competition with the national team—I forget what country we were in—I had an interesting conversation with a fellow teammate, Karen, while on our bus ride back to our hotel. I noticed how happy she seemed, so I wanted to know the reason behind her joy. I felt like all the happiness had drained from my life after the abortion. I was no longer cheerful and high-spirited. Instead, I drifted into a deep depression that left me cold and ill-disposed.

"You're so bubbly," I observed. "What have you been up to?"

"Oh, things are good. I play for an organization called Athletes in Action," she shared. She smiled as she spoke, and as she shared her experience, I could tell that what she had was genuine.

Athletes in Action (A.I.A.), I learned that day, is an organization that was founded in 1966 by Dave Hannah. It is an offshoot of Cru Ministries (formerly known as Campus Crusade for Christ) that purposes to use sports as a platform to help people answer questions about faith while pointing them to Jesus. It didn't appeal to me because it was religious in nature and didn't carry the same recognition and weight that the national team had. However, the more I learned about them, the more I realized that this organization drew people closer to having a relationship with God. Don't get me wrong, A.I.A. was just as competitive as the national team; however, the difference was that we were no longer playing to please our coaches, fans, or even ourselves. We were playing with a purpose that now included God.

———— ◇◇ ————

Athletes in Action offered a fresh perspective to the game of basketball. I had been so engulfed in playing in the spotlight that I had forgotten about the bonding aspect of basketball. After leaving the national team, I had no contact with any of my teammates. I still have connections today with people I played with on the university team, but none with anyone I played with on the national level. This highlighted for me the absence of true bonding and relationship on the national level. It occurred to me that though we'd spent so many years in each other's presence, most of us were more interested in basketball than in each other.

The A.I.A. was different. It was a Christian-focused organization that taught us about the gospel and blending athletics with faith. The leaders taught us how to readily share our faith whenever given the opportunity. They actually merged the rigorous physical aspect of basketball with the intimate spiritual side of each person. We spent a month being trained spiritually before we went on the road to play against other teams.

The team was made up of twelve women who had not previously known each other, but who came together and played beautifully. We blended well because we were all like-minded—we loved the sport and were commitment to God. We were led by a disciple, who led us in daily worship and who spent time teaching us the Gospel, what it means to be a disciple, how to share our faith with others, and how to study the Bible. We travelled across the United States and to Australia together. It was truly a new and exciting experience for me.

———— ◇◇ ————

In 1998, I was invited to attend the WNBA training camp in Chicago. It was an incredible opportunity to be one of the only two Canadian women in attendance. Everyone at the camp was just as competitive as I was. We all wanted a spot in the WNBA and worked hard towards that goal. I quickly gravitated to those who displayed a similar competitive drive for the game as I did.

It was particularly interesting for me to observe the romantic love relationships that existed between the female athletes. I was an eye-witness to several confrontations between my peers due to hurt feelings and jealous emotions. In fact, the strong gender differences amongst the women were more overt than I had previously witnessed in Canada. As I watched, I was careful not to offend those who displayed a more masculine disposition.

The camp doubled as both a tryout and an identification camp to parse through the 'who's who' of the players that showed the most potential. If you didn't make the first cut, you were sent to another tryout in a city closer to your home. In my case, I was sent to Detroit.

Detroit was a second opportunity for me to try out for the WNBA. The scouts in attendance would only be selecting two women out of approximately five hundred to join the team that year. The competition was both tough and surreal. One day during our rigorous draft-training drills, my leg muscles suffered the most painful build-up of lactic acid I had ever experienced in my career to that point. I stopped suddenly, in the midst of performing the drill the coach instructed us to do, and grabbed my leg with both hands. My face contorted with pain as I tried to will my leg to relax. It was useless. I couldn't move another inch on my own. The cramp was more than I could bear. I saw as the coaches frantically beckoned the massage therapist to rush onto the court. When she arrived, she rubbed my leg muscles to dissipate the horrid build up. And the only sound I remember hearing was my own screams echoing through the gym as I writhed in pain. *You can do this, Sue. Just hang in there. You can do this.* I tried desperately to calm myself as the pain coursed through me.

I wasn't selected as one of the two women who would be joining the WNBA that year, so after Detroit, I returned to Canada. I no longer desired to play oversees. I sensed that a new chapter had begun for my life, so I chose to work while keeping myself in shape. Upon my return home, the opportunity presented itself for me to do some missions work. It was just what I needed to get my mind off of the WNBA and all I had experienced in Chicago and Detroit.

I decided to go with A.I.A. on two missions trips, first to Haiti and then to Zambia where we visited fifty cities in fifty days. It was only a few short months after beginning my missionary trips with A.I.A. and learning from them about spirituality that I decided to get baptized. I was baptized in Perth, Australia in the Indian Ocean on a day when the sky was lit by the most dazzling rainbow I had ever seen. The water washed over me with new life as I dipped beneath its surface and emerged once again, brand new. I looked at the rainbow and smiled.

Piece by piece my broken heart was being healed through the ministry of this organization. The shame I had felt concerning terminating my pregnancy, as well as my many failed relationships, was slowly starting to lift. So I decided to hang around for a while.

———— ◇◇ ————

I met Bryon in Ohio at a training camp. He played for A.I.A.'s men's team and I played for A.I.A.'s women's team. He played the off-guard position, and was very fast. We often had to face off on the court during training sessions, but his defensive style was tough to beat. Our first few encounters involved him teasing me about the ring I wore on my left ring finger although I wasn't married. His jovial nature and casual flirtation made it fun to be in his presence. His lively sense of humour expedited the healing that I needed emotionally.

A.I.A. provided a warm family atmosphere because it was centred on Christian values. They made sure that all of us as players felt at home away from home. Bryon and I were often in each other's space. He flirted with me often, but I was pretty much oblivious to his advances because of the brokenness I was dealing with. After months of doing ministry work together and being selected to go on tour in the same group, it finally hit home. Almost a year after we met, I opened up my heart to the possibility of love again and accepted his invitation to go out on a date. For the next two years, our relationship grew from dating to courtship.

After the second year, we were advised by our leaders to diminish the geographical distance between us by living in the same city. Up until that point, I would often travel from Canada to the United States to spend time with him. We talked about what our counsellors advised and decided that it would be easier for me to make the move than it would be for him. The transition wasn't easy. Life as I knew it changed drastically; it was no longer comfortable. I was used to my easy-going suburban lifestyle, but he was from the city, which was rather different. He also had a child from a previous relationship and a completely different family dynamic than I was used to. Instead of panicking however, I would always quiet my fears and speak to myself, *You will learn to adjust, Sue, I know you will.* I promised myself that I would make it work because, for the first time in my life, I had fallen in love.

That year, Bryon proposed to me. I was in between mission trips—I had just returned from Australia and was preparing to leave for another mission trip in a few days. We were in the hotel lobby when he went down on one knee and presented a ring.

"Sue, I love you with all my heart. Will you marry me?"

"Yes! Of course, I will!"

I quickly removed the ring I wore on the ring finger of my left hand and slid it onto a finger on my right hand. My left hand shook slightly as I extended it to him to receive my ring. I was overjoyed. Though marriage wasn't in my short-term trajectory at the time, if I was going to marry anyone, it was certainly him.

Throughout our engagement we had a few disagreements. They all surrounded the living arrangements that had to be made—who would live where, the immigration process, the difficulty involved in relocating, and the list went on and on. Sadly, after only a few months of being engaged, we decided to end our relationship.

It was quite embarrassing, as I had already announced my engagement to the church I was attending at the time. People constantly asked me about the relationship. Everyone wanted to know when the wedding would be. I eventually had to open up and admit to everyone that we were no longer engaged. This was officially the second emotional storm I would have to walk through. The entire ordeal wounded me deeply, and I needed to find something to do with my time immediately. So three weeks after our break up, I left for Cleveland to pursue a Master of Arts Degree with an emphasis in Sports Ministry. I also immersed myself in mission work across North America. Pursuing this second degree and offering aid to the thousands we impacted on our missions trips helped me cope with the broken heart I was carrying once again.

As I look back now, I realize that I wasn't quite ready for marriage at that time. He was a great man of faith, but I wasn't at the place in my life to settle down and be a wife.

Testimony #1

(shared with Athletes in Action women's basketball team)

I had based my whole life on this T-shirt which read "Basketball is life, and the rest is details." I had finally reached the pinnacle of my career. All the sacrifices, hard work, and persistence had finally paid off. I, Sue Stewart, was going to the 1996 Olympic Games. We were representing Canada, competing against the world's best, chasing after a medal. This was it. I'd climbed the ladder of success only to find out it was leaning against the wrong wall.

I worshipped basketball to the point where I knew it would take care of all my insecurities. I, Sue Stewart, was somebody because I played basketball. I was accepted, and so then basketball was my identity, because people could identify me with being a basketball player. To worship something is anything we ascribe great worth to. You see, basketball was something I could totally rely on, it would never let me down, it would always be there for me, and therefore I trusted basketball. And so basketball became my god.

Just two weeks before the actual Olympic Games I was sidelined with a knee injury and was unable to help my team effectively like I was doing earlier in the summer. I had to sit and watch my team struggle throughout the whole Olympic Games with feelings of frustration and helplessness, from the sidelines. Suddenly what was my dream had quickly become my nightmare.

It was after those games that other areas of my life came crashing down. I lost my coach who was very dear to me. From then on, I was mad at the world. I had changed from being the encouraging, motivating people-person to a cold, not-so-nice person. Well, in 1997 I decided to return to the National Team with hopes to redeem myself from a terrible Olympic experience. It was another important summer, and we needed to qualify for the World Championships. Once again, it was a disappointing summer. The only good thing that came out of that summer was that my teammate shared her experience with Athletes in Action (AIA) with me. Then in September I decided that I wanted to go to the USA fall tour with AIA. It was with AIA that I learned how to have a personal relationship with Jesus. In the summer 1995, I had received Christ in my life at church, but I left church not realizing what I had done, and continued living my life my own way.

It was then that I realized that I had worshipped a created thing instead of the Creator of all things. I was building my life around things that can be easily taken away. I needed something permanent and Jesus was that permanent. In Matthew 7:24-27, Jesus says, "Therefore, everyone who hears these words of mine and puts them into practice is like a wise man who builds his house on the rock....but everyone who hears these words of mine and does not put them into practice is like a foolish man who built his house on sand..." like me building my foundation on basketball.

From that experience, I learned that sometimes God's way of getting our attention is by showing us that we have misplaced priorities. Jesus says, "For what does it profit a man to gain the whole world, and forfeit his soul." Sure, it's nice to make an Olympic team, but there is more to life.

*Now I no longer build my life on basketball.
Jesus Christ is life.*

PART TWO
Change in Course

CHAPTER SIX

Broken

───────────◦⟊◦───────────

There was a wicked storm in Cleveland in May 2004. The day of the storm started beautifully, but then somewhere in the afternoon the weather shifted to something dark. I had spent the entire day working with the Fellowship of Christian Athletes as an area representative in North East Ohio. I worked alongside Christian students and teachers from over forty schools, and supported them in their faith walk. I was responsible for providing them with valuable information and resources that would undergird them in their journey and help them grow in their faith. That day had been a particularly long one, but I made it through. As I drove home in the evening, it rained torrentially. It wasn't long before I realized that we were experiencing a storm in the middle of May.

I drove slowly because my car had already been damaged from a minor rear-end collision that had taken place earlier that year when a young woman backed into me in the parking lot of my apartment. Hence, I was extremely careful in order to avoid any further damage to my car. All of a sudden, the unexpected happened. Lightning struck, and it struck my car, leaving it paralyzed in the middle of the road. There I was in my white Mercedes, being carried by the force of my wheels hydroplaning on the flooded street. I was afraid. I feared the worst, but prayed for the best. Somehow, in the midst of my shock, I managed to veer to the side of the road and call a friend to come to my rescue. As I waited alone in the middle of the thunderstorm, my heart beat raced. *God, please don't leave me. Please.* Miraculously, my friend found his way to my location in under twenty minutes, and was able to help get me out of the situation I was in.

Around that time I had begun to feel my time in the United States coming to an end, but I didn't know how soon. There was stress piled on top of stress as I manoeuvred my way between Canada and the United States, back and forth, for school and work. There were great days and there were bad days. Three times I was denied entrance to the U.S. at the border, and twice I was put in a holding cell for questioning. I still don't know what their reasoning was for holding me or turning me away, since I only went there for school and work, but they chose to, and I had no option but to do whatever they said to do. It took a lot of dedication on my part to continue to push through despite the resistance and the strain of the system. I was frustrated, but I also knew that this was all a part of getting to the place of my purpose, so I stuck with it. Almost a full year went by like this—me working and going to school, facing the various struggles that came along the way, and overcoming them one issue at a time. Until something happened that stopped me in my tracks.

April 8, 2005. That's the day my life took a turn I hadn't expected. I was coaching a club team in Ohio called the Swiss Selects, and we were in a tournament. We had just returned to the hotel from a game we played in the morning. Everyone was tired and a bit frustrated because though we had won the game we played the previous night, we lost the game we played that morning. I decided to take the girls back to the hotel to rest before heading back on the road. After giving them a pep talk and telling them how special they were, I went to my hotel room to take a shower and rest as well.

I remember it like it was yesterday. I was standing under the shower with both palms pressed flat against the wall in front of me. The water felt divine. I stood there for a few minutes as my thoughts subconsciously drifted in the refreshing sensation of the water falling on my head and shoulders. I'm not sure why, but I suddenly turned my head to the right.

WHAM!

The side of my head slammed into the metal showerhead beside me. I reached up quickly and gently rubbed the spot I hit. *Ouch! Why did I do that? That's probably going to leave a scar.* There was no blood, just a sharp pain that ran throughout my entire body. I ended the shower and toweled off. I was eager to take my nap before our next game. I set my alarm and called the front desk to schedule a wake-up call. Time was a big deal for me, so I wanted to make sure I was up in time.

BAM! BAM! BAM!

"Sue, what's going on?"

BAM! BAM! BAM!

"Sue! Sue, it's time to go!"

I slowly drifted out of sleep to someone pounding on my door. The sound grew louder and louder as I emerged to the surface of my consciousness. I looked over at my clock and realized, with horror, that hours had gone by since I'd fallen asleep. When I got out of the bed and opened the door, I could see the genuine concern all over the face of the person who was knocking. It was the father of one of the girls on my team.

"Sue, are you alright? We're all on the bus waiting for you."

"Oh, I don't know what happened. I'm so sorry. I must have overslept. I'll be there in a minute." I was embarrassed by the fact that I had slept for so long. It wasn't like me.

I quickly got ready, grabbed my bags, and joined the parents and players on the bus. We were behind schedule because they had been waiting for me for quite some time. A few moments after I boarded the bus, we left for our destination.

As we drove, I felt unusually groggy, but I didn't think much of it. We got to our game, and the sick feeling persisted. *Oh boy, I must've been more tired than I thought.* Before I could finish that thought, and without any forewarning, I started to vomit profusely. It was like someone turned on a pipe. My stomach contents flew from my mouth in an uncontrollable stream. Once again, embarrassment filled me to the core. *What is going on?* That was just the first of four dramatic episodes of vomiting that took place that weekend. Some of the coaches reached over to assist me while the players watched on, shocked. Everyone was perplexed, but none more than I was.

After our final game, a few days later, we went out for a post-game meal. After the meal, we made another stop for desert. Then, as we were waiting for our order to arrive, the vomiting started again. I was beginning to feel worried, but I didn't know what to attribute this sudden bout of illness to. So I got cleaned up, got back on the bus, and headed back to Parkside Church where my car was. Since we arrived early, and my plan was to go to the evening service at Parkside Church, I decided to walk around the Aurora Farms Premium Outlets shopping mall to kill some time. But as I walked through the aisles of Saks Fifth Avenue, the now familiar feeling of nausea began to overwhelm me, again. I ran out of the store to avoid vomiting on the merchandise. I couldn't understand what was wrong with me. I spent the next few hours sleeping in my car. Once I was feeling better, I drove back to the church. My strength was now gone—I couldn't stand, I couldn't lift my bags, and I couldn't focus. I felt cloudy and grey like I was suddenly caught in a fog.

I drove to my home in Canton and arrived a few hours later. I was renting a room near the Pro Football Hall of Fame area at the time. I stumbled into my apartment and headed straight to bed. I remember making two calls before falling asleep. The first was to order food because I had vomited out all the contents of my stomach and was starving by that point. The second was to my mother.

"Hello?"

"Hi, Mom."

"Hello? Is that you, Sue?"

"Yes, Mom, it's me."

"Why do you sound like that? Are you okay?"

It was then that I realized that my speech had begun to slur quite badly. I decided to keep the conversation short so I could get some sleep.

"I'm not feeling well, Mom. I think I'm coming down with the flu. I've been vomiting all day. But I'm going to get some rest now."

"Okay. Make sure to drink some fluids. I'll call and check up on you."

She called me every hour on the hour to check up on me after I made that call. I could always count on her. After lying in bed and sleeping for what felt like hours, I felt the need to go to the washroom. So I mustered up the strength to get out of bed at that point. The delivery person had come with my food a while earlier, but I was too weak to answer the door, so I simply went without food. As I stood facing the bathroom mirror, still weak and groggy, I observed how sickly my eyes looked. *What is going on?* Then suddenly, just like so many other times that day, the room began to spin around me. Before I knew it, my legs gave way beneath me and my body fell backwards and crashed onto the bathtub and shower curtain that were behind me. The back of my head landed squarely on the metal soap dish that was affixed to the wall of the shower. Pain coursed through my body like heat; only this time it was worse than the hit I sustained in the shower a day earlier. This was bad. Something was broken, I was sure of it. My roommate, who was in the other room at the time, heard the commotion and came running. When she saw me lying there, sprawled across the bathtub half-conscious, she panicked and dialed *911*. Before losing consciousness, I asked her to hand me the phone so I could call my mother once more.

"Mom, I just took the whole shower curtain down." My

speech had gotten worse. The words were barely audible through my slurring.

"What happened? Did you put a dent in the tub?" My mother joked. She didn't yet realize how seriously I had injured myself.

"No, Mom. It's bad. I hit my head. It hurts."

I couldn't articulate my injuries much more than that. I just knew that the pain was terrible, and I was losing consciousness.

It was April 13, 2005.

As I rode in the ambulance to the hospital, I thought about all the plans I had made during the week with the intention of carrying them out that weekend. I was scheduled to attend my second interview with a church in Canton, Ohio that wanted to hire me as a Christian Education Minister. My first interview had taken place a week earlier and it had gone so well that they invited me back for a second meeting. I was really looking forward to getting that job because it meant transitioning to the States full-time and filling a position that appealed to my skills. But as I laid there in the back of the ambulance, I felt the opportunity slipping out of my grip like a runaway ball. I knew I wouldn't make it for that second interview. Next I thought about the pastor who had prayed for me the week before when I had visited my friend, Shauna, in Cincinnati, Ohio

"In two weeks your life is going to change, young lady," he prophesied. But what did that even mean?

Finally, I thought about my roommate who, just a few days ago, had spontaneously demanded that I give her my emergency contact information in case something ever happened to me. Well, something did happen. I just didn't know what it was yet.

It's not lost on me that if I'd only told someone earlier that I'd hit my head in the shower in the hotel room that maybe I would've gotten the immediate help I needed. Maybe they would have known that I was suffering from a concussion. Maybe, I wouldn't be lying on a stretcher, surrounded by nurses and strangers, being read my last rites by the hospital chaplain.

They are preparing for me to die! The thought scared me. I had everything lined up and going in the right direction before I hit my head against that showerhead and again against that metal soap holder. But all my plans didn't matter now; my life was about to change forever.

I slipped into a coma.

CHAPTER SEVEN
Life on a Gurney

Why can't I move my eyeballs? Oh my God! Why can't I move my eyeballs?

Everything seemed unreal to me. I was now lying in a hospital bed when just a few hours earlier I was on a basketball court cheering on my team. I laid there watching as people walked in and out of my room. I was helpless. My vision was so blurry that all I could see were shadows. I was paralyzed from my neck down. And I couldn't even move my head; it was limp, so they propped it to one side with a pillow. To make matters worse, I also had a tracheal tube in my throat, and I was being fed through a tube in my stomach.

I couldn't understand what was wrong with me. I felt like a pile of bones had replaced my body. My hospital room was crowded with well-wishers and encouragers, yet I was the loneliest I had ever felt in my entire life. My pastor came to visit and pray with me, as well as other pastors, Fellowship of Christian Athletes (FCA) members, Christian friends, and members of A.I.A. They told me that my brain was bleeding and that it needed to stop in order for me to be flown back to Canada. Apparently I had bruised my brainstem when I first hit my head on the showerhead followed by the second hit on the soap dish in my hotel washroom, which worsened the damage exponentially.

"The brainstem is a very sensitive part of your body," they explained. "Once it isn't functioning properly, it is a long process to repair it."

I was anxious to get out of the bed and regain my independence. But I had a feeling deep inside that the journey ahead would be a long and arduous one. All I could do was pray and trust in God.

———————— ◇◇ ————————

I stayed in the hospital in Canton, Ohio for a whole month. For that first month, my mind was in overdrive. It was the only thing that hadn't been impacted by the accident, so my thoughts flowed rapidly and incessantly as I laid awake in bed. I could feel my body being bathed by the nurses, and I struggled in my mind because I would've preferred not to have to go through that. But I was helpless. I couldn't protest, and I definitely couldn't lift a limb to bathe myself, so I had no choice. Throughout this time, my medical bills started to pile up since I was not an American citizen and had no medical insurance. My family and friends had no other option but to raise money to take care of my surmounting medical fees and airlift me back to Canada. My church in Canada decided to organize a concert to raise funds, and my family and friends contributed what they could. Thanks to those sources, my medical bills were paid, and by mid-May I was finally transferred to Trillium Health Centre in Mississauga, Ontario. It was known for its work with patients who'd suffered brain injuries.

My mother accompanied me in the helicopter for the flight back to Canada. I was constantly aware of the sounds and the activity around me throughout the flight. But I felt trapped in my body in the midst of the excitement. I couldn't raise my head, I couldn`t move my limbs, I could only see and hear. My mother made sure to communicate with me throughout the flight in order to keep me abreast of the progress, and also to make sure that I understood what was happening. It was the scariest few hours of my entire life.

When I arrived at the hospital in Mississauga, I still had the tracheal tube in my throat and the feeding tube in my stomach. My vision was still impaired; I could only see in one direction. I couldn't speak, so I communicated by using my fingers to sign *Yes* or *No*. I felt like there were IV tubes connected to every inch of my body like a string puppet. As my visitors piled in, I watched as their eyes watered at the sight of my body laying paralyzed in the bed. It was there that I met Nurse Jackie. She was like my personal angel sent on duty to take care of me.

My visitors were instructed to "gown up" before entering my room for a visit because the medical team was concerned for my well-being. They stressed the utmost importance of me not contracting any viruses from the outside while individuals came in and out of my room.

My mother shone like a star in the sky on a dark night, not only because of her warm attitude, but also because she intentionally wore bright colours to her daily visits. My eyes were so drawn to the colours that they would follow her around the room. She said she wore the colours as a sign of life and hope. She knew that it wasn't time to be dreary and to demonstrate sadness, but rather to keep me alive and hopeful that everything would be okay.

She diligently washed me on every visit to ensure that I was clean according to her standards. My hygiene was her first priority—she used a sponge to clean my teeth and scrub my tongue. If I didn't look my best, she would make sure to fix that before she left. She demanded that I consumed my meals, even when I didn't feel like it. She even massaged and stretched my legs daily, and when she couldn't do it she would ask a nurse or someone else to do it. She knew that because I was paralyzed, my limbs needed extra attention. And after a long day at the hospital, she would secure a hand roll in each of my hands—a ball of wash cloths rolled together and taped around each palm—to ensure that my fingers would have something to curl around and hold on to while she was away.

One night when Mom slept over in my room, I had trouble sleeping. I was terrified to be alone at night so she would sometimes sleep over to keep me company. On that particular night, I felt extremely bored as I laid awake. My mother was fast asleep, so I decided to entertain myself by pressing the buttons on the side of the bed to move it up and down like an elevator ride. It was fun to feel the movement since I had been stuck on my back for more than a month. I wanted to test its limits and go as high up as I could. "Bzzz..." the bed buzzed as it moved towards the ceiling. When the ceiling was but a few feet away, I heard a click. *I guess that's as far as it goes.* I pressed the arrow down button to return to the normal ground level, but nothing happened. I pressed it again, and squeezed it harder. Still nothing. *Oh my God, I'm stuck!* I couldn't quite speak yet, so I was terrified. I stayed up there, next to the ceiling until my mother eventually woke up.

"Sue? Sue, are you okay? What are you doing up there?" Her tone quickly went from concern to panic.

The next sound I heard were her feet scurrying to get help. A nurse ran in a few minutes later, but she was nervous and unsure of what to do to return the bed to its original state. They had to call in a technician who then fixed the bed and brought me back down. Needless to say, I never entertained myself that way again.

Mom was my champion of hope on my saddest days. She would intentionally keep the music playing, so that my room was filled with the sound of worship music, day and night. The atmosphere was so uplifting that even my nurses expressed how happy they were to come to work each day and experience the life that filled my room. There was one particular day when I felt like I wouldn't make it. I was asleep for most of the day, in and out of consciousness. But every time I woke up, I would see my mother from the corner of my left eye (the only eye that worked at the time) deep in fervent prayer. I would hear her beseeching heaven on my behalf. There were times I would awaken to her interceding by my bedside for me to be healed, for me to live. She held on to the gates of heaven, and cried out with all her faith to God. That image stuck with me as I faded in and out of consciousness that day. Her passion infused my thoughts and shook the last bit of hope I had to the surface. I know that I am alive and well today because of the faith she embodied and the relentless prayer she offered up for me. She saw to it that I held on and braved the harshness of the fight for my life.

Some days my emotions were raw. I had gone from being a world-class basketball athlete to a frail brain injury patient confined to a bed in a hospital room. My emotions and thoughts were my only independence at the time, and so they flowed incessantly. I oscillated between hope and fear, worry and regret, uncertainty and courage, and occasionally silence. Sometimes all in one day. Sometimes from week to week. It depended on how the day started, how my body responded, and what I could see and hear.

I often called for Nurse Jackie because she quickly became my favourite nurse. Our spirits connected almost instantly the moment she first introduced herself to me. Every time she entered my room, she greeted me with a smile. She shared the same faith I did, so she would often do Bible study with me at my bedside and pray with me. I called for her around the clock. She was like my safety blanket during my stay at the hospital. She came every time I called, and she never seemed annoyed or bothered. I met many friendly nurses throughout my stay, but Nurse Jackie won my heart. She cared for me like a close friend and ensured that I was as comfortable as I could be in the condition I was in. Between Nurse Jackie, my mother, the physical therapists at the hospital, and the visits from my family and friends, I started to improve more quickly than expected.

—— ◇◇ ——

Rehab was no joke. The first part of the rehabilitation process entailed getting me out of bed. I had been lying in bed for more than a month at this point, so my muscles had lost all of their strength. The doctors ordered for me to be taken out of bed once a day so I could sit upright. In order to get me out of the bed, the nurses had to put me onto a hoyer lift and then lower me onto a chair. At first, I was asked to sit in the chair for at least twenty minutes. I hated it. It was so uncomfortable that I would start calling for the nurses to put me back into the bed a few minutes after they got me into the chair.

The next step was to learn how to stand from a seated position while holding onto a bar in front of me. I didn't like this step either. At first, I could only sit and stand two times in a row. I felt awkward. My muscles were incredibly weak, so it took all the strength I could muster to coordinate my limbs to achieve this one action. And though I was weak all over, my left side was much weaker than my right side. By then I had also lost a lot of weight since I was only consuming puree and liquids after being taken off the feeding tube. Finding the stamina to sit up in the wheelchair and eventually stand was a hard task. But I did it.

Next was speech therapy. I had to learn how to speak again. I had to learn how to undulate my voice in order to carry out a normal conversation. I also had to undergo occupational therapy, which taught me how to hold a pencil and move it up and down in order to write a letter of the alphabet. My hand felt strange, as though it wasn't mine. My struggle was so obvious that my six-year-old nephew, who often witnessed my failed attempts to write, actually said, "It's okay, Auntie, your hand is just dumb." His description pretty much summed it up. It was hilarious how his little mind computed what was going on with my dexterity.

When they finally removed my tracheal tube, the doctors and nurses asked me to try to chew a piece of bagel. The thought alone was frightening because I hadn't chewed or swallowed anything solid for close to two months. So I approached the assignment slowly and fearfully, biting off a tiny piece at first and chewing it slowly. Then, finally, I swallowed. My mind buzzed with thoughts as the morsel coursed down my throat. *What if I choke? What if it gets stuck?* But it didn't. It went down with ease. After that, I was able to reintroduce solids into my diet.

After a full month in the hospital, I had made considerable progress—I was able to transition myself from my bed to my wheel chair, stand while holding onto a bar, and eat solids. By the end of June, I was discharged from Trillium and transferred to another specialized health care facility called Toronto Rehabilitation Institute.

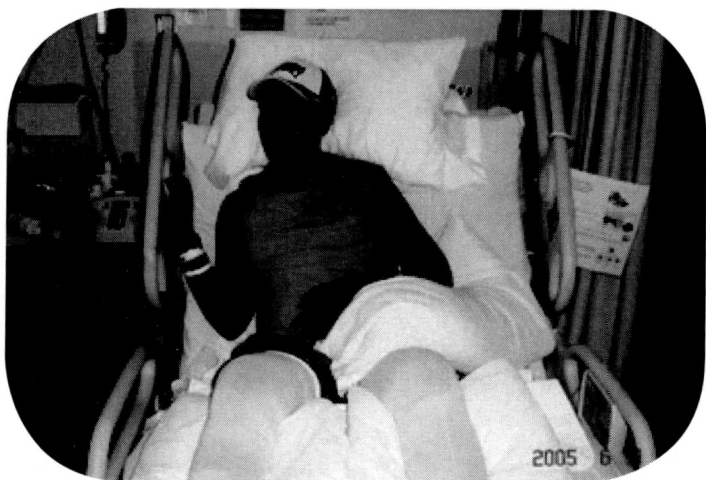

CHAPTER EIGHT
The Path of a Heroes

A t Toronto Rehab I met some of the most amazing people in healthcare. They were precious gifts to me on my journey to full recovery. When I first arrived at the rehab facility and realized that there were four people assigned to each room—in my room there was one lady whose bed was surrounded by books, there was an Asian lady who spoke no word of English, and there was another lady who wore a helmet all day—I cried and told my mother that I wouldn't be able to survive there. When the nurses saw my reaction, they decided to transfer me to a different room. My new room had patients who were in my age group. One was a former reality television show contestant, and another lady had multiple sclerosis and couldn't move any of her limbs. I was surrounded by people who had head injuries, which made me even more antsy to get better.

I made it a part of my routine to visit the prayer room often to pray. This quiet time of meditation kept me hopeful and encouraged whenever I'd start to feel down. I also got involved in all the social and religious programs they offered at the facility, including Bingo. It was a different environment from what I'd become used to, so I did all I could to adjust as I healed. Thankfully, there was a certain porter who transported patients to their rehab sessions who would sing "Hallelujah" as she walked up and down the halls. Her song carried with it a sense of familiarity that made me feel more comfortable with my surroundings. I loved how cheerful and upbeat she was; it helped me settle in.

The first time they came to shower me, I resisted as much as I could verbally. My privacy concerns had returned now that I was no longer entirely immobile. But I hadn't yet relearned how to shower, dress myself, tie my shoes, or even walk. Furthermore, my left hand had stiffened into a tight fist that rested on my chest. It was difficult getting it to straighten and open up to do activities. So I had no option but to give in and allow myself to be showered by these strangers.

My biggest challenge in rehab was learning how to walk up and down the stairs. Surprisingly, walking up the stairs was the easier feat of the two. Once I got to the top of a short flight of stairs, my brain, my leg muscles, and even my hands had no clue how to coordinate in order to get back down the stairs. It took attempt after attempt after attempt to get it right.

I saw physiotherapists, occupational therapists, recreational therapists, and speech therapists. The physiotherapists were responsible for teaching me how to walk again. They would ensure that I went for daily and nightly walks, even when I didn't feel like it. They took me on walks within the compounds and outside of the building. They also made sure that I walked on many different surfaces—on tiles, on carpet, on concrete, on grass, and on the asphalt of the sidewalk. Eventually, I graduated from using a wheelchair all the time to using a walker and then to using a cane. I walked all the time, every day. I walked holding on to parallel bars, I walked holding a tray, I walked holding a bottle; it was never ending. But it helped me heal faster.

The occupational therapists were responsible for making me functional again. They would teach me everyday things that I once took for granted, like how to make my bed, make a cup of tea, fold a sheet, do laundry, and how to get dressed. The recreational therapists were responsible for making me active in a social setting. At one point they had me playing wheelchair basketball, which they thought I would enjoy, but I hated it. I was an Olympian who was used to jumping and scoring, I couldn't quite adapt to playing from a chair. Then finally, the speech therapists were responsible for teaching me how to speak again. They engaged me in reading stories, memorizing those stories, and answering questions about them. They taught me how to form my words and coordinate my mouth with my brain to get the sounds out right.

But even after I passed each stage of therapy, I wasn't allowed to be discharged until I could prove that I was able to live independently. So in my third month of admission, the doctors ordered that I be moved to an independent-living penthouse on the top floor of the institution. There they would visit me and ask me to make myself a salad or a sandwich. It was challenging, but I also knew that I was nearing the end of my stay, so I pushed myself to do whatever they asked for.

The staff was on a rotational schedule, so I didn't have the same nurse all the time. However, they were all supportive and caring towards me. After three full months in the rehabilitation hospital, I was discharged to live with my parents. I was ecstatic to leave, but I knew the journey to full recovery was not yet over. In fact, I remember my Aunt Bev saying to me upon my discharge, "Now the journey begins, Sue." Her words resonated with me as soon as she said them. I felt extremely proud of myself for achieving that level of progress, but there was still so much that I had to learn to do in order to successfully thrive in the outside world.

———— ◇ ————

When I first arrived home, I looked at the stairs and knew I wouldn't be able to climb them. For about two weeks, I slept downstairs, gathering the strength to make my first trip upstairs. My vision was still impaired to the point where I couldn't look out the window while I rode in a car; it was dizzying to see all the objects whiz by. I also couldn't listen to radio programs because they sounded too loud, and the noise would bother me. Not to mention I still felt like I needed the back-up support of my wheelchair. Nevertheless, after two weeks, I mustered the strength to ascend the stairs to my old bedroom. I hadn't seen my room in years, so I was curious to see what it looked like. Especially since while I was in the rehabilitation facility, my parents and sister had driven to Canton, Ohio with a U-Haul to pick up all of my belongings, including my car, and bring them back to Mississauga, Ontario. I felt like a champion the very first time I made the trip up the stairs, though my body screamed something else.

One day, my sister and I decided to go to the mall. When I exited the car and my sister drove off, instead of going up the small ramp as I was trained to do, I decided to step up onto the curb. I'll never forget what happened next. My legs buckled beneath me and my body collapsed, sending my cane flying through the air. I screamed in panic because I was afraid of being injured again. Fortunately, two women who were standing nearby ran to my rescue and helped me back onto my feet. I didn't sustain any injuries that day, but it reminded me that my healing was a process that didn't make room for shortcuts.

After leaving the Toronto Rehabilitation Institute, I moved on to receive outpatient care at another hospital. I relied on the TransHelp service offered by the city to get to and from my appointments. Depending on the transit system was a new experience for me since before the injury I was used to getting around on my own. But I could no longer drive myself, and no one could predict when I would ever be able to drive again, so I had to face reality and sell my car. Sadness swept over me the day I made the decision to sell my white Mercedes. My sadness wasn't just about losing my car, but more so about giving up that last piece of my pre-injury norm. It stung hard. After that, I knew I had to adjust to being entirely dependent on others to get around.

The outpatient care involved more sessions of rehabilitation activities. I now did Tai chi, swimming, stability ball classes, muscle relaxation techniques, aqua-fitness, and chair classes. I did these activities for three years, nonstop, as I trained my body to become functional and efficient once again. Irrefutably, the journey I was on was not a journey for cowards, but one for the brave at heart. And I wasn't afraid. After all, that kind of bravery had a familiar ring to it.

Testimony #2

(shared while working with the Fellowship of Christian Athletes)

◇◇

My name is Susan Stewart. I'm thirty-five years old and a 1996 Basketball Canadian Olympian. I have achieved consistently high results, optimal levels of personal performance, and received many awards and recognition for my contribution to the sport of basketball and my community.

I recently completed my Masters in Christian Ministries with an emphasis in Sports Ministries at Malone College in Canton, Ohio. While attending Malone College, I was a graduate assistant with the women's basketball team. My current medical condition has not allowed me to remain in Canton because I had to move back home to Canada to be in my family's care.

On April 8, 2005 while coaching the Swiss Select girls' basketball team at a tournament, I began experiencing what I thought then were flu-like symptoms. Prior to the start of the tournament, I had an accident while taking a shower, where I slipped and hit the side of my head hard on the shower head. But I shook off the pain because that is what athletes are told to do while showering at a hotel. Throughout the basketball tournament, I was vomiting profusely and found it challenging to focus on the games.

The vomiting continued for the next few days and my day-to-day routine activities were compromised as a result of my accident. But that didn't stop me from going to Chagrin Falls, Ohio where I attended Parkside Church. Although I wasn't able to stand up for praise and worship, my focus remained on the Lord. After service I was faced with a one-hour drive to Canton, Ohio where I lived.

On April 13, 2005, I fell again when trying to go to the washroom. I hit my head against the soap holder in the bathtub. I didn't realize it at the time, but this second blow caused further damage to the brain stem. At this point, I wasn't feeling well. My roommate called the ambulance at Mercy Medical hospital and notified my parents of the accident. They drove from Canada to Canton, along with many friends and family, to be with me.

The doctors had told my parents that I had suffered a brain aneurysm and that they weren't optimistic of my survival. I was heavily sedated, unable to speak, open my eyes, eat, or even breathe on my own. After a few days of watching me in this condition, my family requested to have the sedation and codeine drip seized. What comes next may seem impossible, but the week April 17, 2005, I flat-lined (died) and then came back to life about twenty minutes later. That was the beginning of my rebirth. "For I know the plans I have for you, declares the Lord" (Jer. 29:11)

On May 4, 2005, I was airlifted from Mercy Medical Hospital and flown to Canada where I was admitted to the Mississauga Trillium Health Centre with a brain aneurysm. After receiving treatment, I was able to breathe on my own, eat without the feeding tube, gain some strength on my left side (partially paralyzed as a result of the fall) and communicate with family and friends.

With much improvement, I was then moved to the Toronto Rehab Institute. Tremendous improvement was made and I was discharged on August 25, 2005. I am now an out-patient at the Credit valley Hospital.

Today I'm able to help myself, walk without a cane, speak more clearly, and one day I will play basketball again.

Sue with the Next Step to Active Living staff

CHAPTER NINE
Life's New Purpose

My time spent in all three institutions was very humbling. All those months of hospitalization taught me the value of human love and care, and what it meant to rely on someone else for all my needs, including my bath. Therefore, I knew without doubt what my next step would be; I was going to give back to my community in whatever way I could.

As I neared the end of my out-patient care, I was asked to speak at an elementary school as the country prepared for the 2000 Olympics. The school was looking for a speaker to address the children and give them some insight on what it meant to be an athlete. I loved the experience. It sparked something within me that I hadn't felt in a long time. Subsequently, I met a teacher who was looking for a coach for the Streetsville Secondary School girls' basketball team. I quickly accepted the offer as this was my opportunity to encourage young women to think highly of themselves and be all that they can be. I wanted these young ladies to experience the same healthy self-esteem and confidence that sports brought into my life. After coaching at Streetsville Secondary for a year, I was asked to be the assistant coach for the senior boys' basketball team at St. Aloysius Gonzaga Secondary School. Once again, I was extremely grateful for the opportunity. And thankfully, those weren't the last offers I received.

After my tenure with the boys' team, which lasted about a year, I started to look for a full-time job. My case worker told me about the Coalition for Persons with Disabilities and how they help people with disabilities and injuries prepare for the workforce. I engaged in the hands-on training they provide by working at one of their satellite offices. The satellite office existed to train people through the use of real life situations. After my training, I became an intern with Cosmo Sports, a sports marketing company for sports teams. I worked as a sports executive. I chose to do an internship since I was eager to get back to work, but had not yet secured full-time employment. One day, while on-site at my internship, I saw a job posting from Ryerson University for volunteer basketball coaches. I immediately investigated the opportunity and met with the athletic director at the university. During our meeting, he encouraged me to get back into coaching, which sounded like music to my ears. I applied for the position, and got the job as the assistant coach for the women's basketball team.

I spent a year there. I was coaching again, and it felt great to be back on the court. The basketball court was home to me. It made me feel alive. The whole experience was exhilarating.

I moved on to the University of Toronto the following year as the volunteer assistant coach for the women's basketball team. Although I had a better experience there, I was not able to land full-time, paid employment with them either. I treasured the experience of working with the young athletes, and only wished I was able to do more for them as they reached for their dreams to play on a national and international level.

By this point in my recovery, not only was I coaching, but I was also doing regular speaking engagements at local high schools and rehabilitation centres across Canada and the United States. I was often called on to speak on my experience as a brain injury survivor. Other times, I was called on to speak to young athletes who were heading to the Olympics. I loved those assignments. For me, it has always been about giving back. I knew that everything I had learned throughout the course of my life could be used to benefit the many young athletes who were aspiring to make it to the top of their game.

My struggle to land a full-time paying job also lit a flame within me to advocate for other people with disabilities who are discriminated against. There is value in people that can sometimes be veiled by their physical ailments. My inability to successfully reintegrate into the workforce has been humbling, especially when I consider the fact that I have become somewhat of a hostage to my condition in other people's eyes. I dream of being completely financially independent once again. I dream of imparting the knowledge and experience I have amassed into the lives of youth who aspire to reach a level of greatness. I dream of one day being given the chance to do what I know I can do in a professional environment to affect change, not just as a volunteer, but as a valued employee.

To this day, the Mississauga Sports Council continues to keep me involved with the sports in Mississauga.

Today I spend my days speaking with anyone who'll listen about the power that exists within us to overcome the difficulties and challenges that life hands us. As for my physical status, my vision is still impaired, and I have now been diagnosed with astigmatism, which was induced by the injury. I'm still working on improving my balance, so my mobility is not yet at the place it used to be pre-injury. I find that I have to exercise twice as much as I used to in order to keep my weight in check since I'm not able to run. The left side of my body is weaker than the right, and sometimes both sides go out of sync with each other completely. I feel much less agile than the woman I was those days leading up to the accident. But I'm not discouraged.

Despite the physical challenges I face today, my spirit and my mind are intact. I don't allow my limitations to define me because there is much more to me than what I can do with my arms and legs. I have always had an innate confidence that I can do anything if I put my mind to it. For that reason, I have never walked around afraid or ashamed of what has happened to me. Nevertheless, I am very cautious. I calculate all my movements at all times to avoid falling and hurting myself again.

There is no time limit on healing; it is a process that is different for every person dealing with brain injury. I have sincere gratitude for everyone who has helped me during my process of healing. There is so much that I want to do with the life I have left, but transportation has by far been my biggest challenge. Hence, I am especially appreciative of systems like TransHelp that have helped me to be mobile, and get to and from my appointments. It hasn't been easy learning to depend on the goodwill of others in certain critical areas, but I am sincerely grateful for the help I get in doing those things that I am still unable to do for myself.

I know that my full recovery is imminent.

Conclusion

◇

on't take anything too seriously. Bad things will happen on this road called life. Things will not work out, things will get broken, things will get lost, you will have rough days, and you will cry. It's okay to cry. I cried many times over as I faced the difficulty of the road I would have to travel. I cried when I couldn't remember how to feed myself or how to walk down a flight of stairs. But my tears had meaning, and only served to push me harder.

There are still days when I feel let down by those around me—family, friends, peers, and even random strangers. I've had people talk down to me because of my disability. Yes, I slur when I speak and have a limp when I walk, but that doesn't mean that I am less intelligent. I have had to correct the insensitivity of others in public spaces who have tried to capitalize on my physical disadvantage. I refuse to present myself less than I truly am. I am still a person; my personhood has not been diminished by my injury.

Be Sensitive

I lived on Sir Lou Drive in Brampton for a year and a half amongst people with disabilities. I was placed there by the Brain Injury Association of Peel and Halton. While there, I heard the stories from many other individuals who were suffering from a brain injury of some sort; many of them were heartbreaking. We have to remember that it doesn't take much for a person to feel alone and unsupported. We are emotional beings; that means we were hardwired to feel love.

If there is someone in your life who is dealing with a disability of some sort, don't withdraw from them. The loving presence of others is of utmost importance to the emotional health of that individual. Just because someone slurs when they speak or walks a bit differently doesn't mean that they are stupid, so to speak. There is no need to speak louder or slower to them, unless, of course, they are hearing impaired. Don't enunciate as though it is necessary to sound out all the letters of each word, unless it is expressed that that is what is needed. It is easy to hurt the feelings of someone who has a endured a physical as though but is being treated as though she has a psychological defect.

Furthermore, don't be afraid to include a recovering individual in your social circles. I have never felt as lonely as I have felt since my injury. I've found that people avoid hanging out with me. They hesitate to include me in some of their social gatherings. For the sake of the thousands of others out there like me, remember to be kind and sensitive to those who find themselves on the recuperating side of life.

Be Grateful

Appreciate the small things in life. Being grateful helps

us to be happier people. Remember that the important things in life are not the things we can buy, but rather the things we've been blessed with. Never take life for granted. Live with passion. Live on purpose. And be thankful for the people in your life who help you to be better each day.

Be Positive

I've come to realize that there will always be negative people in this world. There will always be someone who will try to bring you down, but don't give in to their words. Listen to those who encourage and push you to reach your goals. This may sound cliché but that's because it's true: Believe in yourself.

Have Faith

Throughout my journey, my faith in God was truly tested. The Bible verses, *"I can do all things in Christ,"* *"In Him we live, move, and have our being,"* and *"It has been granted unto us to suffer,"* became real to me. I drew on their truths and used them to overcome. I learned what it meant to trust in God in the darkest places of life. I learned to trust Him when I went from being a champion on the court to not being able to move my limbs. It was cultivating my faith in God that sustained me. I learned to spend time praying and reading the Bible in order to strengthen my relationship with Him. And as a result, I developed the mind of Christ. My days weren't easy. I still asked God "Why me?" every now and then, but His presence kept me and comforted my anxiety.

You too can use your faith to weather the storm. Allow God to give you His strength in your weakest moments. I never would have made it if it wasn't for God. His strength became my strength. His power became my power. As you read this book, know that He loves you just as much as He loves me. In fact, He wants to do great things in your life.

Take Up Your Cross and Follow Him

I have often wondered what it meant when Jesus said to his disciples, *"If anyone would come after me, he must deny himself and take up his cross and follow me"* (Matthew 16:24).

Today, Christians view the Cross as a cherished symbol of atonement, forgiveness, grace, and love. But 2000 years ago, in Jesus' day, the Cross represented nothing but torturous death. When Jesus carried His Cross up Golgotha to be crucified, the Cross meant one thing and one thing only—death by the most painful and humiliating means.

I now know that "Take up your cross and follow Me" means being willing to die to my flesh in order to follow Jesus. It's a call to absolute surrender. Jesus said, *"For whoever wants to save their life will lose it, but whoever loses their life for me will save it. What good is it for someone to gain the whole world, and yet lose or forfeit their very self?"* (Luke 9:24-25). Although the call to follow Jesus is tough, there is no greater reward.

Following Jesus is easy when life runs smoothly. But our true commitment to Him is revealed during trials. Jesus informed us that trials will come to His followers (John 16:33). But always remember that God will never give you any trial that you cannot pass. There aren't many people who would respond to an altar call at church that went, "Come follow Jesus, and you may face the loss of friends, family, reputation, career, and possibly even your life." But such a call is what Jesus meant when He said, "Take up your cross and follow Me." However, following God doesn't mean that all these things will happen to you. Rather, commitment to God simply means sacrificing the pleasures of the world and laying down your idols for the cause of Christ.

Turn to God

God wants to know you personally. As humans, we are sinful and separated from God. Therefore, we cannot know and experience God's love and plan for our lives without first turning to Jesus. Jesus Christ is God's only provision for sin. Through Him you can know and experience God's love and plan for your life (John 3:16). The way to receive Christ is by personal invitation. Simply invite him in with your words. God says, *"Behold, I stand at the door and knock; if anyone hears My voice and opens the door, I will come in to him"* (Revelation 3:20).

Giving your life to Christ is a big decision. In that one step you are asking God to erase all of your sins, and to make you a new person. If you have come to the decision that this is what you want to do, pray this simple prayer, asking Jesus to come into your life, and He will.

"Jesus, I know that I am a sinner and need your forgiveness. I believe that You died on the cross for my sins and rose from the grave to give me life. I know You are the only way to God, so now I want to quit disobeying You and start living for You. Please forgive me, change my life and show me how to know You, in Jesus' name. Amen."

PART THREE
APPENDIX:

Personal Accounts
FROM FRIENDS AND FAMILY

Nona Stewart
(Mother)

Since Sue was a little girl, she adored sports; any kind of sport would do, as long as it was active. She loved to play, and she especially loved to compete. She had that toughness about her.

I knew she would be a champion one day. She would always watch basketball on TV; she especially admired Magic Johnson. One evening as she was watching a game on TV, she turned to me and said, "Mom, one day I'm going to play with those people." And I thought she was kidding. I remember telling her high school teacher that I was concerned about her school work. I told them that if her grades were being affected by the sports, then I would have to pull her off the team. But her teacher encouraged me that she brings so much pleasure to people when she plays that it would be better for her to stay in than be pulled out. She later went on to have a very successful career in the game of basketball. I am that I had allowed her to be herself and maximize her potential.

The Injury

When Sue came back to Toronto from Ohio in the air ambulance, we didn't know the extent of the injury just yet. We actually thought that her brain had just become overwhelmed by all her studies. As we spoke to each other, over her bed, about the injury, she suddenly came out with, "That's not what happened." Her speech was very slurred, but we understood what she said.

Anywhere she went for rehab, the staff loved her. She was a stickler for time because of her years of training in basketball. Therefore, she was frustrated whenever people would be late for her appointments. She was also a big encouragement to the other patients to the point where family members and staff would ask that she sit with the other patients and speak with them about her story.

She was always determined to push her limits. If they asked her to hold on to the bar and stand five times, she would say, "No, I'll do seven." They had never encountered anyone like that before. The hospital and rehabilitation staff admired her and loved her.

The Future

There is a future for Sue. She is a woman of faith, and she is very determined and hopeful that full recovery is in view. For that reason, I am also confident that her future is bright, and that she will continue to touch countless lives with her story.

Jordan Fairback
(former roommate)

I met Susan in August of 2004. She and I had entered the Sports Ministry program together at Malone College. As is par for the course, my first impression of her was that she was really tall. But that was quickly overcome by her obvious sweet spirit. Susan and I had several classes together, and I remember being amazed by her eagerness to learn and apply her education. She was motivated, disciplined, and intuitive in her studies.

Susan and I bonded mainly over the love of basketball and the Lord. We church-hopped a little bit together, but she was far more extroverted than me and willing to network. I often followed her tail wings with people and her involvement in local ministries.

Shortly into the new year of 2005, Susan moved into a small house with me and Stephanie Ash (now McPherson). It was a small three bedroom close to campus. Although Stephanie and I had lived together for several months by ourselves, we knew Sue would be an easy roommate and a good friend. One of the first things we started to do together as a house was workout. Whoa. Talk about determination! Susan pushed my body to new limits. Although I figured she was in shape from being an Olympic athlete, I had no idea the drive she had to push her body. I was in pain for months. But I loved it, and was thrilled to have someone motivating me to a new physical level.

During the month of April, there was an opportunity to attend a sports ministry conference in England. I jumped at the chance to go, and was thrilled that several of my classmates would also be attending. Due to Susan's strenuous coaching schedule, she was unable to attend. I promised to take notes and pictures for her.

I think it was my third day at the conference that I was checking my email and received one from a fellow classmate asking me if I was okay and how Susan was doing. I had no idea what she was talking about. I quickly did my best to get a hold of Stephanie to find out. I think I managed to Skype her and get her on her cell. Stephanie then began to relay the series of events that taken place in the house. I was shocked and saddened and angry to not have been there. That evening, I quickly found my professor and conference leader and shared the news with him. I remember being up on stage that night with a circle of people praying for Susan's rapid healing. We were heartbroken for our friend.

As I flew back to Canton, I was both nervous and anxious for what was to come. After I landed, Steph immediately took me to the hospital. I was overwhelmed by the presence of her parents, cousins, and all the people that loved her. I can vividly picture her lying in the bed, eyes closed, with tubes everywhere. Ugh. My heart sank. At this point they knew she would be okay, but that a very long recovery was ahead.

For the next several weeks, Steph and I had family in and out of our house, and we were in and out of the hospital. We would visit often; usually we would pray with her. One of her favourite things to do was sing, which she did so poorly ☺. I would bring my guitar and Steph and I would worship next to her. Occasionally, she would tap a finger to the music, which made our hearts soar. Her mom would always be right beside her.

One of the highlights in the hospital was a graduation ceremony held for Susan. Malone waived her uncompleted assignments, and brought a tasseled hat and diploma to the hospital bed. Her mom dressed her up, put make-up on her and did her hair. It was a sweet time of celebrating her achievements and saying goodbye before she was taken to Canada.

A few months later, Steph and I trekked up through Niagara Falls to see her in Toronto. She was still in the hospital at this point, but had slowly begun to talk, eat, and do physical therapy. It was wonderful to see progress, as slow as it was.

Although I have not seen Susan since then, she has always stood as a role model of perseverance for me. She is a fighter. Her love and trust in the Lord never wavered. She has used every step of this journey for His Glory, and I stand amazed. It has been an honour and a pleasure to be in her life.

Jacqueline Green

I have known Sue Stewart for thirty years. We first met in high school (Streetsville Secondary School) in 1985 when Sue was in grade nine, and I was in grade twelve. I remember watching Sue play in her first high school basketball game, and I was quite impressed by her skills. We immediately connected. Although we never played on the same high school basketball team, we would often practice together, showcasing our skills. I never told Sue this, but I secretly wished I could play basketball as well as she could. I truly admired her talent. In my year book, the year we met, Sue wrote:

> *Jackie, this year I am glad that I have met you. You have been a great friend and I hope it lasts. Have a great summer.*
>
> *Friend 4-ever,*
>
> *Luv Sue*

It was Sue who actually introduced her family to mine. Both families have remained close to this day.

Sue and I have two interests in common—our love for God

and our love for basketball—in that order. It's our commitment to serving God and our love for basketball—and sports in general—that keeps us connected.

Basketball

Although Sue and I played on separate high school and university teams, and coached in different capacities, and Sue's basketball talent led her to be a part of the Canadian Junior National and Olympic teams, we always remained connected. In 2001, Sue invited me to be part of a women's basketball ministry coaching program in Muskoka Woods. Not only were we expected to help develop the women's basketball skills, but to also share our faith and study the word of God with them. This was the first time Sue and I had ever coached and ministered together. What an amazing experience that was!

God

Sue and I have always attended different churches and have been a part of different ministries. But our belief remained the same—we believe in the same God and serve Him in the same way. Through each challenge, success, high and low points in her life, it is her love for God that has kept her faithful and strong. Sue is very conscious of the fact that the ultimate purpose of her life is to glorify God in all that she does. 1 Corinthians 10:31 reads: *"So, whether you eat or drink, or whatever you do, do all to the glory of God."* She knows that above all things, through any struggle or persecution that may come her way, it is her duty to think about how she can glorify God in those situations. Even when we thought Sue had died in April 2005, it was her strength and determination that brought her back to us. Sue's life story shows just how God continues to use her talent and skills, her love and commitment, her faith and strength to touch many lives—as God wants all men to know Him and to serve Him.

God and Basketball

Throughout Sue's basketball career, she always asked herself the question, "How can I glorify God in the way I play basketball?" She started playing basketball at a very young age, so you can only imagine the number of hours that she has spent learning the sport—in the gym, in the classroom, and travelling abroad. She was amongst people of all religions, cultures, morals, and work ethics. I'm sure she was faced with temptations of all sorts, including her own selfish ambitions. As a Christian, I know there are times when we forget about God, especially when our own selfish tendencies take over. But there were many humble moments that Sue was reminded that her talent came from God and not man, and that she needed to use that talent to glorify Him, both on and off the court.

Colossians 3:23–24 reads: "*Whatever you do, work at it with all your heart, as working for the Lord, not for men, since you know that you will receive an inheritance from the Lord as a reward. It is the Lord Christ you are serving.*" Sue knows that scripture quite well and knows that God calls her to do everything in life for the glory of God, and not for people. She has always strived to be all that God created her to be. When she's feeling lazy, judgemental, or apathetic about the things she does in life, be it ministry, studies, or even basketball, she is reminded of that scripture. Whenever I watch Sue play basketball, there is a tremendous freedom in knowing that when she plays, she plays to glorify God. She doesn't play hard because she has something to prove or someone to impress, but because she is playing for God.

Sue's basketball confidence wasn't always at an all-time high. Things didn't always go well for her in practice and in the important games. There were times when she struggled to produce points or play her best defensive game. She had to continue learning and growing as an athlete, and in her weakest moments she had to rely on God for strength, wisdom, and encouragement. Not all of her teammates were Christians, but it didn't change the fact that they had modeled Christ's love to her through their support and encouragement. Her teammates loved her and enjoyed playing with her. She was an inspiration to many of them. If Sue were to ever play basketball with Jesus, I don't doubt He would encourage and uplift her the same way that her teammates did.

I thank God for bringing Sue Stewart into my life. She is a loyal and faithful friend, a great athlete, a wonderful daughter, sister, aunt, and sister-in-Christ. Praise God for inventing sports for us to play! And praise God for teaching us how to love Him by bringing women like Sue into our lives.

Herbie Kuhn

<hr>

Sue and I have been friends going back twenty years. I call her "Stew," so that's his automatic default name. Herbie met Sue in 1995, she was playing for the Canadian national women's team and I was announcing at McMaster University for the 1996 qualifiers for the Olympics. Canada and Cuba were playing, but the Canada clinched that victory over Cuba, which was considered the powerhouse at the time. Stew played a major role in this victory, and that's the first time she registered on my consciousness.

Our paths criss-crossed in several different ways in the basketball circles. It seemed that every couple of months, or several times a year, between the late 90s and early 2000s, we would see each other—at games, at a church, or at a ministry or outreach event. Stew was one of those people who, even if you didn't see her all the time, you still remained fantastic friends; that was just her personality.

In February 2000, Sue and I did a missions trip to Haiti with A.I.A. I had just started in full-time ministry for the first time in January of that same year. I was part of the A.I.A. team led by Bob Johnson. The team consisted of about eight people— members of A.I.A. staff and volunteers. Sue was the only female on that team. We were a bunch of testosterone-filled guys, and then there was Sue. She was at the height of her basketball prowess, playing on a national level in Canada.

We went all over the island of Haiti. We were allowed two pieces of luggage; each team member was required to take one suitcase for their personal use and a hockey bag filled with sports equipment donated by National Sports. Wherever we went, the goal was to leave behind a few pieces of sports equipment and bless the people. We wanted to bless those communities tangibly with the equipment and spiritually with the word of God. We did a week of soccer, basketball, and baseball instruction in different schools and camps, and left equipment for the kids along the way. Sue and I tag-teamed preaching and teaching. I remember speaking the most French on the team, though my French isn't all that good. So Sue would preach in English and I would translate. What an incredible privilege to serve Christ alongside a remarkable and incredible woman. We had a blast!

We were a bunch of middle-aged guys, decent athletes, but if it was not for Sue we would have been humiliated on the court, playing three-on-three with Haitian teenagers. She was our saving grace. She would hit eight-foot jumpers, so basically our game plan was simple: get the ball and pass it to Sue. She took 75%–80% of our shots.

I remember one particular instance where we visited a school and played a soccer game. The field was behind the school, and our team played against Haitian students. Again, Sue was the only female on the field. Even though it was a male-dominated trip and environment, Sue actually scored a goal. Due to the cultural dynamic, a lot of these kids were humiliated that a female had scored on them, and the team had to find a fine line between wanting to razz them and celebrate, but also be gracious guests and empathize with them.

That's a memory that will always stand out in my mind about Sue on our trip to Haiti together. We visited school assemblies and ministered to many young people. I also remember the laughter on that trip. The fact that the eight of us hadn't known or met each other beforehand didn't matter. The camaraderie and the laughter that took place was amazing, we were like a family. Bruce Compton, a retired firefighter from Pickering, was our driver on the trip. Their roads were almost like Steeles Ave. West in Toronto with all the potholes, which had us hankering for a chiropractor after the trip.

Sue and I have also been on radio together, we've been on TV together, and have travelled together. I had the privilege of having a radio show on Voices for Life Cafe Joy1250, which lasted for about two years or so. I would bring a special guest to interview, and Sue was my guest on that radio show. She was always one of those people who would always be available and ready to speak.

Yes TV (formerly CTS) at one point had a long-running show by Paul Willoughby called Night Light Live that aired from 1:00 a.m. – 5:00 a.m. Paul asked me to host the show once while he was travelling, so I decided to have Sue on the show for an episode. She was always gracious and generous with her time.

When she was in the U.S. coaching, she suffered her brain injury. I remember being at home when I got a call from Nona, Sue's Mom, telling me that Sue was in a coma in a U.S. hospital on life support. She was basically fighting for her life. Nona asked me to pray, and we both prayed for God to intervene and deliver her.

I remember sitting on the edge of my bed with a cordless phone in my hand, weeping with sorrow that this lady with so much athletic talent, fervour, and spiritual strength was on the cusp of losing her life. I remember saying. "Lord, please help. The doctors can only do so much, and we humans can only do so much, but we need to see You do something."

However, I didn't get to see her until she was transferred to Trillium in Mississauga. I made an effort to see Sue as much as I could due to my flexible schedule. God laid it on my heart to be consistent in her life and visit Sue in the hospital frequently.

As I walked into that hospital room for the first time, I tried not to allow what was going on in my heart to show on my face. I tried to look strong, compassionate, and confident, and to speak in a gentle voice. But what I saw was a woman hooked up to tubes and wires, with flickering eyelids, barely able to communicate.

I will never forget leaving the hospital thinking how precious life is, how blessed we are, how we take it for granted, how we swing our feet off the bed every morning, saying, "What's on my schedule to do today?" without a second thought for how blessed we are. Stew's condition was a major nudge for me to value the blessings and gifts that each day brings. Even though Sue never asked to be that nudge in my life, God used her to teach me that.

I began to visit Sue at Trillium at least a couple times per week. At the time, I was living in the beach area near Queen and

Woodbine. So it was a thirty-five-minute drive on the Gardiner Expressway through Etobicoke to Mississauga, and there were days I didn't feel like battling traffic. But then I would hear a voice inside me say, "Herbie, your friend is incapacitated in a bed and you're in a comfortable car, so get your backside in your car. You have the time to go see her, so go! This is not about you, it's about God."

I felt that God wanted me to speak to her in a calm voice, so I kept on visiting. During these visits I would have many interactions with her family members, and I would have an opportunity occasionally to pray with them as they watched their daughter, niece, auntie struggling in that bed.

After her stay at Trillium, they moved her to Toronto Rehab on University Ave. I kept on visiting. In a world of uncertainty, where she didn't know what obstacle and/or blessing was around the corner, I wanted to be a consistent representation of Christ's love. I remember pushing Sue around in a wheelchair and encouraging her, trying to get her out in the fresh air or in the sunshine.

I watched her progress. It was really amazing. It was hard to see her go from the loud, confident woman who could be heard in a crowd to a woman who couldn't do anything for herself. However, she worked hard and was blessed with medical expertise, and God used those people—the doctors and nurses—to bring her out of this deep valley that she had found herself in. I watched her learn to speak again, to feed herself again, and take her first steps again.

Eventually, after a period of time, we celebrated when they moved her into one of the Independent Living units on the

twelfth floor. Sue had autonomy and the opportunity to survive on her own. Maybe a week or two after she had to demonstrate her ability to live there, she came through!

More than anything, over and above all these circumstances, was her mindset and perseverance. Death and life are in the power of the tongue. We can speak negativity into the situation, or positivity into it. We all have the mind of Christ, and Sue's determination and positive mindset, positive speech, and positive outlook were a powerful determining factor in her recovery. I don't recall her ever pitying herself. Never heard her ask, "Why me?" or "Doesn't God know better?" She always believed that something amazing was around the corner through this situation.

This was evidenced by all the graduations and milestones that occurred along the road of her recovery. First, she graduated from the American hospital and was able to make the trip back to Canada, she then graduated from the Mississauga hospital, then she graduated from the Toronto Rehab facility, next she graduated to the twelfth floor Independent Living unit, and then eventually returned home to be with her family. Now look at her. She's unstoppable. She's coaching basketball, she's ministering to individuals. She's preaching, teaching, sharing her testimony wherever she can.

Stew's the kind of person who I would want in my corner. If you want to liken life to a boxing match, she's the one I would want encouraging me and inspiring me between bouts. And I have no doubts that she will be in my corner, speaking life and lifting me up with the power of her encouragement when I need it. I know that if I picked up the phone and needed her –

she would be there for me.

I look back at all the time that I spent at her bedside, encouraging her, ministering to her, supporting her, and praying for her. It was not a hardship; it was an investment into the life of a spectacular person and child of God. It's such a privilege and my life is better for it; my life has greatly improved as a result of Sue Stewart and spending my time and life with her. She's a powerful lady.

Anyone who knows Sue knows that they've been touched by a child of God. That's the power that she walks with, and she has inspired thousands and thousands of people with her testimony.

Steve Nash, two-time MVP who plays for the L.A. Lakers, and Sue knew each other from the Canada basketball program in the mid-90s. After her brain injury, but also after she had graduated from rehabilitation, I saw Steve at some point during the season and told him what had happened to Sue. Steve was extremely disappointed and very saddened to hear of Sue's injury.

When Steve Nash came to do a charity event in Toronto to a sold-out crowd of about 19,000 people, I arranged for Sue to be there. I got her backstage passes, and when Steve was coming off the court, I quickly informed him that Sue was here and told him to hurry a little and meet us behind the locker room. I remember Steve changed as quickly as he could, and before the media were allowed into the locker room, we went to a side room where Steve and Sue could have a chat. And I had a front-row seat watching these two great athletes talk.

What stood out for me was that even though Sue hadn't

seen her long-time basketball buddy in a while, she wasn't sharing her complaints as to why this happened to her or why she had to struggle. Instead, she took the opportunity to give God praise for His faithfulness through her entire ordeal. Steve Nash was at the height of his career at that time, a superstar. And even though it was clear that Sue had been significantly slowed by this injury, she seized the opportunity to give God the glory for bringing her through. I'm sure if someone asked Steve, he might remember this meeting.

This was just another great example of Stew using one of the most adverse situations someone could go through to let God's light shine in the world of professional sports.

Sue is one of the best people anybody could ever hope to know.

André Thornton

I was introduced to Susan through Gordon Heffren, the Chairman of the Board of Fellowship of Christian Athletes (FCA) in Ohio. Susan was working for the group that Gordon was overseeing. He asked me if I would be interested in meeting and supporting the efforts of Susan in that FCA region, and I said "Yes, I'd be happy to do that." Susan also attended our church, and I remember meeting her and greeting her. We went out to lunch and she shared some of her background with us as well as some of her goals and what she wanted to accomplish with her work for the Fellowship of Christian Athletes.

She mentioned that she was looking for a place to stay, and we knew that she was new to the area. We had a one-bedroom cottage on our property, so we told her that she was welcome to use that cottage for as long as she wanted, until she got her feet on the ground.

Having been athlete for many years in world-class competitions, Susan exuded a sense of confidence, had a lot of energy, and was very excited about the future. Even though she wasn't quite sure what the future would hold, she had this abundant confidence that she had a lot to give in the future. We all sensed that tremendous confidence and excitement she had about having something to offer and give back. I'm sure a lot of that came out of her Olympic experience and her athletic prowess, but it was like a young person who was beginning to see all of the vast opportunities before them, and I saw that sort of excitement inside of her to reach out and grasp them. Another reason why it was so easy to help her was because of that enthusiasm, excitement, and readiness to take on all that the world might put before her.

A friend of ours who was the State Coordinator and Chairman of the Fellowship of Christian Athletes in the state of Ohio called us and alerted us to what had happened to Susan down in Malone. That was a week or so after the accident. We were devastated when we heard the news, especially as dire and as touch-and-go as it was at that time. When we first heard what happen to Susan, the pain was a deep pain. We had a chance to go down to the hospital to see her after a while. But it was gut-wrenching, painful, and sad. I felt sorry for her because I knew how difficult the road of recovery would be.

When I went to the hospital, she didn't even resemble the Sue that we knew. It was a person who was incapacitated, for the most part, and recovering from a very traumatic incident. We tried to encourage her and let her know that she would be on the minds and hearts of everyone. I don't remember her responding, though she was awake. Her responses were very muted, and her speech was slurred.

From the treatment standpoint, her mother decided to take her back to Canada since there was nothing more the hospital in Ohio could do for her. It became a matter of rehabilitation, but I wasn't privy to those types of talks, though I did speak to her mother briefly. But, again, we just learned later that she had gone back to Canada and was under the care of her mother and family.

Sue was a lovely person, and it was a desire of ours to be as helpful to her as we possibly could, and we were happy to do so. Certainly, for us it was a sad day when we heard about her accident and the ordeal that she had to go through and was going through over these many years. Our prayers are that she would be healthy, and that the Lord would restore her health, and that her testimony would ring true.

She called us one day and told us more about what had transpired in her life post-accident. I remember that she was very upbeat on the phone and that it was very encouraging when contrasted with the initial reports of her accident. She was starting to come around and things were looking a lot better.

Everything happened so quickly in a truncated time period, but I remember Susan as a bright star, and we were very happy to be a part of her life during the time she was in the United States.

Beverley Harvey

Sue has been friends with my children since grade three, and their friendship is what brought our two families together. I see Sue as being strong and very caring at the same time. She also has a great sense of direction. From an early age, she seemed to be the 'son' that the family never had, in that she was very athletic. She fell in love with basketball, and it became her life as she blossomed at the sport. We supported her at her games in high school all the way through to university. I also watched as she committed her life to God and began to use her sport for ministry.

When I found out Sue had suffered an injury, my daughter, Michelle, who is like a sister to Sue, and my goddaughter, Denise, were on their way to visit her in Ohio. She was still unconscious. They had actually received a call from the hospital saying that she had passed away. But before they arrived, they got a second call saying that she was still alive but unconscious. It was such a moving time. No one knew if she was going to make it. Sue was not able to control her head, so it was leaning to one side. I was able to stand by her bedside and support her head as the media came in to take her picture for the newspaper.

It is a miracle really, the fact that she survived. She was such a fighter. She rallied through her recovery. I remember that during prayer, even when she couldn't speak, she would attempt to participate by making slight gestures with her hand.

Today she has come such a long way, and she has never wavered from her faith and trust in God. Sue is a very positive person, and she continues to reach out, even in her disability, to help youth and other people.

Nurse Jackie Nugent

I was there when the call came into the hospital asking whether or not she should be transferred to Trillium, and I remember yelling, "Yes! We have to! I know her."

When she arrived, I entered her room and spoke to her. She was conscious, but she couldn't communicate verbally. I knew her prior to her injury because we attended the same church (though we were not close friends), and I was aware that it could present a conflict. So I made her aware that I was assigned to be her nurse, and asked if she was okay with that. She responded "Yes," through her non-verbal method.

She was completely debilitated. When she arrived, it was a direct transfer, and I was working on our stroke unit at Trillium. The only thing she could do was blink her eyes and squeeze her hands. But I saw the spirit of resilience within her. She pushed herself to the limit. She had the incredible ability to stretch herself. She was determined not to quit. You could see that she knew she had too much to gain to quit. I admired the determination she had to recover. During her stay at Trillium, the Olympian in her came to the surface. That's what I saw. I saw the champion training and saying, "I'm not gonna give up." This inspired me to create an award in her name called the Stewart Spirit Award that is given by my non-profit organization to a person within the community who displays a spirit of determination and community outreach.

Looking after Sue was refreshing. She has a beautiful Olympics tattoo that stood out in my mind. It spoke to how much going to the Olympics meant to her. I learned that although she was not on a basketball court, she was still a champion in the hospital bed. I've never seen anything like it. I also remember her mother staying by her side, never leaving her an inch. I saw the strength of family come alive in them. She was like a security blanket for Sue as she protected her environment and atmosphere.

My time caring for her brought deep meaning to the work I do as a nurse. I realize that we don't know much about people until we spend intimate time with them. Her faith, her worship, and her spirit kept her going and that was an inspiration. She left a vivid imprint on my life.

Kristin Presley

Susan was my daughter's coach for her AAU basketball team. Susan accepted the role as coach and the girls and all the parents were thrilled when that became a reality! Susan loved the game of basketball, had an impressive history, loved the Lord, and was a great example to the girls.

We went away most weekends for two months in the spring. I enjoyed being with Susan, and I can remember her and I sneaking away to Walmart to get things we needed and loving every minute I spent with her. She was fun and funny, and I was impressed by her work ethic. She was in school working on her master's degree at the time, was coaching the girls, and was also involved in other ministries and activities.

The day of the accident we were all on the bus ready to go, but Susan was not outside yet. That was so unlike her, so my husband, Pat, went to her room and knocked on the door. Susan did not answer after several knocks, and Pat called me on the bus and asked if she had come out. We all became very concerned because we did not know where she was and why she was not answering. After pounding on the door and eventually screaming her name, Susan came to the door. Pat said she was groggy and incoherent. Susan stated that she was feeling dizzy and ill. Her demeanor had totally changed; she was not her happy, smiling self. She got to the bus with Pat's help and tried very hard to be herself.

At the game she started to throw up uncontrollably. We were convinced that she had the flu because she continued to throw up throughout the weekend. The whole experience shows us how strong Susan really is because she continued to function for the whole weekend while being sick. Cindy and I both begged her to come home with either of us so we could take care of her, but she refused.

When she eventually woke up from her coma, we were amazed. It truly was a miracle. She was not the same person. I am a nurse, and she had all the typical symptoms of a traumatic brain injury. She did seem to understand everything, but she was limited in her responses. It was nonetheless a joyous occasion to have her regain consciousness.

Dianne Norman

I have known Sue Stewart since the summer of 1988. I am an East-coaster, and was coming into try-outs for the National Development Team. I always found these situations tense, so I was astounded to hear laughter, and not just regular laughing, but the best guffaw ever! There was one individual that was out shooting threes and laughing and joking with the other athletes who were still tying up their shoes on the side-lines. In a rather stressed environment, she was having a blast. I must say, watching her confidence and the way she tossed up threes with surprising consistency all while chirping, made you want to have her on your team. I later discovered that this cracker-jack comedian was Susan Stewart, who quickly became known as Stewey.

As our first practice got under way, the battle between the guards started. The guard positions are the hardest positions to crack on the national squad. Stewey seemed oblivious to the fierce competition and the intensity of that position as people fought to gain or protect a spot. Eventually, we ended up on the same scrimmage team. As the whistle blew for the next line, she looked at me and said, "Let's go, Norman!" And that was it, we were buds for life. Over the years, I heard that phrase hundreds of times. Whether it was getting ready for a night out on the town, or coming down the hall in a training camp, or yelling across the court before a game, or travelling in another country, I could hear Stewey before the doors opened, "Where is Norman? Let's go, Norman!" I always went, because when you went with Stewey, it was never, ever boring.

We were heading into first year university that fall. I had yet to choose where I was going. Like Stewey, and most of that class, we all decided to stay in Canada. My heart was set on University of Toronto, but my math was lacking, so that was not going to be a reality, and I was sorely disappointed. Those were the days before text and cell phones and computers. One day, I got a call on the family dial up phone. It was Stewey saying she had decided to go to Laurentian, as did some of her Ontario buds. I had never been to Sudbury, but had met Peter Ennis, the coach, that summer and thought he was wonderful. I needed to make a decision because time was running out. So I asked if I could be her roommate if I went, to which she replied, "Yes." So without even a visit or knowing the school colours, I headed off to the Big Nickel. And Stew was absolutely right about the fun we would have; those were some hilarious times. Good thing it was in the days before social media.

Moving to Sudbury from the East Coast was not much of a cultural change for a New Brunswicker, I am not sure I can say the same for my Torontonian roommate. I noticed she started to wear my hand-knit mittens by mid-September. My mom then sent mitts and a tuque for Stewey, so that when it actually became cold in November I had something to wear. Stewy kept on wearing a tuque as long as she possibly could. In 1989 in Sudbury, in Stewy's opinion, there was no place to get her hair done. So she routinely went back home to the experts, and she did not want to ruin her hair with a silly hat. The great thing about those trips was when she would bring back an amazing care package of Jamaican patties and other delights, which I loved. Then one day, I was returning from class, and I saw my tuque coming along the trail; she was going to class. That pompom was hard to miss. Before I could even open my mouth to comment, out came her one finger, which was covered by my mitts, waving back and forth (that finger was waved at refs, people who offended her, players who tried to chirp, impolite fans, after she drained a three, so I became well acquainted with that waving finger) "Not a word, Norman! Not a WORD." Starting to wear a tuque was Stewey's final resistance to the way of the north. From then on, fashion was secondary to her warmth.

Our adventures were numerous and filled with hilarity, embarrassment, learning moments, and life changes. I cannot reflect on my university days, my national team experiences, or the Olympics without Stewey being a central figure. When she retired from ball, I felt a huge gap and loss. Her retirement came shortly after our beloved coach, Peter Ennis, died. At that point, I had been playing with her for twelve years. We had been through the guts and glory of international sports together, and supported each other through several personal hurdles. I can unequivocally say that I would not have been able to succeed and persevere through the diversity we encountered if it had not been for Stewey's consistency, humour, relentless drive for success, and *joie de vivre*.

I was home in New Brunswick studying for my master's

degree when I got news of Stewey's injury. At that point, we were not seeing each other as often. Stewey retired from ball, but I had continued playing. I am not even sure I know who called; it might have even been email at that point. I was devastated. We were told she would not make it. I should have known she would prove them wrong, everyone wrong.

I had the opportunity to speak to Stewey once on the phone while she was in the rehabilitation hospital, and remember trying not to cry when I heard her voice. Inevitably, I did and proceeded to sob uncontrollably when I hung up. Despite being warned ahead of time, it was a shock to hear the voice of the single most gregarious person I have ever met sound so weak and garbled. Eventually, I was able to visit her, and I took her out on an outing. She was living at home at this point. We went to a coffee shop, and she told me her story. She explained how hard it is to navigate curbs now. She described a trip to a store when, because of the problems with her vision, she had fallen. I responded in a sympathetic voice, "Oh, Stewey, I am so sorry. That must have been so hard." I was assuming she would have been embarrassed to fall in public. But Stewey looked at me like I had three heads and said matter-of-factly, "Norman, people fall." Stewey had a long way to go at that point, but she was in there and she was slowly coming to the surface, again. She was winning. And it was not long before she started waving that finger, again.

Links and Resources

◇◇

- **Athletes in Action:** *http://athletesinaction.com*

- **Fellowship of Christian Athletes:** *http://www.fca.org*

- **Peter Ennis Biography:** *https://www.basketball.on.ca/ site/content/Peter_Ennis1.pdf*

- **Praise Cathedral Worship Centre:** *http://praisecathedralwc.com*